COMMUNITY TECHNOLOGY PROJECTS

MARGARET HELLER

COMMUNITY TECHNOLOGY PROJECTS
Making Them Work

Editions

CHICAGO 2019

MARGARET HELLER is Digital Services Librarian at Loyola University Chicago. She has been active in library technology communities, serving on numerous planning committees and the LITA Board of Directors. She is the author of many articles and blog posts about topics including open access, web development, digital collections and services, and inclusion issues in library technology.

Extensive effort has gone into ensuring the reliability of the information in this book; however, the publisher makes no warranty, express or implied, with respect to the material contained herein.

ISBNs
978-0-8389-1837-1 (paper)
978-0-8389-1858-6 (PDF)
978-0-8389-1860-9 (ePub)
978-0-8389-1861-6 (Kindle)

Library of Congress Cataloging-in-Publication Data

Names: Heller, Margaret, author.
Title: Community technology projects : making them work / Margaret Heller.
Description: Chicago : ALA Editions, 2019. | Includes bibliographical references and index.
Identifiers: LCCN 2018059752| ISBN 9780838918371 (print : alk. paper) | ISBN 9780838918586 (pdf) | ISBN 9780838918609 (epub) | ISBN 9780838918616 (kindle)
Subjects: LCSH: Libraries—United States—Automation. | Libraries—Information technology—United States. | Library cooperation—United States. | Computer specialists in libraries—Professional relationships—United States. | Library information networks—United States. | Communication in library science—United States. | Libraries—United States—Automation—Case studies. | Library cooperation—United States—Case studies.
Classification: LCC Z678.9 .H436 2019 | DDC 025.00285—dc23
LC record available at https://lccn.loc.gov/2018059752

Book design by Alejandra Diaz in the Expo Serif Pro and DIN typefaces.

♾ This paper meets the requirements of ANSI/NISO Z39.48-1992 (Permanence of Paper).

Printed in the United States of America
23 22 21 20 19   5 4 3 2 1

To my sisters, Elizabeth and Abigail,
with whom I formed my first community.

CONTENTS

One evening in February 2009, I opened the door to a small storefront on the side of a large theater building. The room was filled with a big table, and the walls were lined with shelves of paperbacks and zines. This was my first look at the Chicago Underground Library (now known as the Read/Write Library Chicago), which was founded as a grassroots independent library in 2006 to bring together works by disparate artistic communities in Chicago. I was fresh out of graduate school at the University of Illinois Urbana-Champaign, having graduated in May 2008—at the same time as a massive economic downturn. After a disheartening job search which had ended in part-time work with bad hours, I was attracted by the idea of a library I could make my own.

During my first volunteer meeting at the Read/Write Library, I got so excited about the project that I agreed to migrate the website to the Drupal content management system to create a new kind of library catalog, which I accomplished over the course of the next year. Over that year and in years following. I kept showing up to perform activities such as staffing the space during open hours, scrubbing the toilets, filling out the IRS paperwork, and developing the website. This work led to new professional opportunities, but more important, it gave me a vision of what a library community could be and the amount of work it takes to make one successful. I remain on the board of directors, even though I am less hands-on these days.

The library is still attractive to new volunteers today precisely because it offers an appealing community experience and showcases the ways in which Chicago—still a city divided by race and class—can come together. Working with the Read/Write Library Chicago helped me feel empowered to bring that same sense of community and do-it-yourself approach to my day jobs and to the other groups with which I have worked throughout my career.

My empowerment has translated well to participating in technology communities, including stints on boards, working groups, local technology meetup groups, and conference planning committees, as well as posting on social media about digital collections. Participating in these many ways has given me firsthand knowledge of how library technology communities work. What I have learned is that the work is done by those people who show up and keep showing up. This is true of library work in general, but specially so for technical projects. Some types of library work have decades (such as MARC cataloging) or centuries (such as bibliography) of consensus on how they should be performed. Consensus is still in the making when dealing with tools or projects that have only existed for a few years. Active engagement in communities that are creating new tools and practices is the only way to stay current and to help shape those tools and practices.

In any type of library and any type of job, library workers rely on rapidly shifting technology. Everyone must be aware of how to get help or give it, ask for changes, and shape best practices. Everyone needs to develop skills to become comfortable engaging with communities, finding appropriate leadership roles, and maintaining sustainable and positive communities. The problem is that for many people, even those who want to be part of the work, it can feel impossible to discover how to get started in technical communities. I wrote this book because I have had many conversations with people who see communities they admire but cannot figure out how or where to get involved.

This book is a guide for people who want to get started with community technology projects, understand what their options are, learn how to find and create communities, and decide which skills to learn. For those who are already engaged with communities, it will be a guide to creating a welcoming community for new people and maintaining a motivated community in challenging times. I want everyone to be inspired to make better library technology communities.

I am very grateful to the Loyola University Libraries for allowing me so much time and latitude to work on this book. Thanks to the many colleagues at Loyola, and in particular Hong Ma, who were understanding about my need to shift projects around to complete the work.

All my communities were essential to this book, both in teaching me how to be a member of a community and by listening to my ideas as I have worked through them over the past few years. My LITA and Code4Lib friends and colleagues who have worked to improve those communities have been especially educational and inspirational. I appreciate that the women of LITA who make up so much of my professional support network never allow me to leave any idea unexamined.

Thanks to my editor Patrick Hogan of ALA Publishing for asking me to write this book and for providing helpful guidance throughout the process. I can hardly thank Chris Martin enough for his help with the book, for reading the manuscript and always being willing to listen.

And last, but certainly not least, thanks to my husband Mike Birnbaum for his many excellent suggestions and forbearance with my challenging schedule. My parents and parents-in-law were instrumental in the process, providing weekend childcare and helpful advice. My children, Ira and Julian, gave up many hours with me so I could work on the book.

CHAPTER 1

WHAT SUCCESSFUL COMMUNITIES DO

■ Definition of Community

Community projects are about people working together to solve a problem. Successful communities become so because the appropriate people have found each other, identified a problem, and figured out some solutions to it. Community technology projects may suggest a certain type of development and collaboration—for instance, a distributed network developing open source software. But because of the nature of library work, I use the word "community" more broadly, as encompassing *any technology project with a collaboration between multiple individuals and/or libraries or library-related organizations.*

Library technology communities can take many forms. A collaboration can be as small as an informal group in a single city, or as large as an international association. It can be a formal entity with a board of directors, or a group that exists primarily via an e-mail list. Communities such as user groups or support networks can form around commercial projects. Large associations such as the American Library Association or Society of American Archivists have divisions and sections focused on technology issues. And certainly, many library technology communities take the form of open source software developed by distributed networks.

Communities go in cycles. Communities may start small, become large, and then break apart into smaller communities. They may remain stable for years, only to experience upsets in funding, staffing, or mission, which, once resolved, restore stability. Choosing the appropriate techniques or tools at each stage of the cycle can be a challenge. The life cycles of community projects were illustrated in *It Takes a Village: Open Source Software Sustainability* (LYRASIS 2018), a recent guide to open source sustainability for projects related to cultural heritage and scientific information. According to this model, life cycles are a series of phases and facets. Phase 1 is "Getting Started," Phase 2 is "Growing/Getting Established," and Phase 3 is "Stable but Not Static." Within each phase are facets, which are specific considerations for the project. For open source technology projects, this guide identified for the following facets that will apply to any technology community: governance, technology, resources, and community engagement (LYRASIS 2018). We will return to these ideas throughout the book as we consider various types of communities and see how successful communities adapt and evolve.

■ How I Researched This Book

Over the years during which I have worked with library technology projects, I heard certain stories about practices that worked or failed in community projects. But were these true? To test my impressions, I looked systematically at community-oriented projects in library technology that had been presented at national conferences over the past decade. My data included thirty-three projects, of which twenty-one are still active. I then expanded my examination to the larger bodies that sponsored these conferences or engaged community in other ways, and I explored published case studies about projects with a community focus. I grouped communities into four categories: small-scale distributed development projects, user groups, general technology associations and consortiums, and large-scale distributed development projects. The types of projects include discovery layers, bibliographic management systems, library technology management tools, integrated library systems, content management systems, infrastructure networks, and community libraries or support networks.

At first, I assumed that successful projects would share factors like external funding, professional staffing, or strong adherence to the same mission over the years. Instead, I found successful projects could be entirely self-funded, volunteer-based, and willing to shift mission or focus as needed. Nor did the size of community or type of project seem to matter. What successful communities have in common is that they support their members both technically and emotionally. I tracked the types of support various communities offered and explored what the unsuccessful communities may have lacked. However, sometimes a community may have done everything right and still have been unsuccessful due to changing technical realities. It may have faced major challenges, as, for example, when an institution that employs the project's developers no longer supports their work on the project. Nothing about developing an open source community is easy. Several case studies will help to illustrate the nuances of how communities run into problems.

■ What Successful Communities Need

It takes work to maintain communities. The process of creating communities requires clarity about what is important, dedicated effort to maintain that clarity, and a willingness to change or adapt over time. It necessitates setting aside individual egos in favor of larger ambitions while still ensuring that the community adequately meets the needs of its participants. Most communities fail when an individual vision, or a vision shared by only some of the members, is not meaningful to the group. Communities that grow and evolve require setting aside preconceived notions and sharing a vision that is compelling enough so that all involved will show up and do the work and keep showing up.

Communities need to have strong values. Community is especially important in libraries, because the mission of libraries includes sharing, which necessitates trust. For that reason, we must be particularly careful to create communities that are not exclusionary or exploitative. Some communities have failed or are at risk because of unethical practices. There are communities that are still active but have bad reputations. We are at a critical juncture in our society as we grapple with newly revealed history of institutions covering up unsavory behavior. We must assume libraries and library technology projects are not immune to these risks, and work to improve our own institutions.

Communities need to support their members. Working with others on technology projects—or any complex projects—requires mastering the complex interplay of personalities, ambitions, and knowledge. Success or failure is dependent upon a multitude of external factors over which the participants may have little control. Companies go out of business, grants end, and institutional priorities shift. Despite those realities, the individuals who make up a community have their own perspectives and desires. Helping people find engagement within the community helps weather changing times.

■ Using This Book within Communities

I intend this book to address many levels of interest in community projects, but three groups of people will find specific content to meet their needs: participants, managers, and funders. Many readers will fit in multiple categories (e.g., people who work at funding agencies might participate in technical communities out of personal interest).

> » Participants want to get involved with a community, whether for an existing or new project. Throughout I will point out avenues for engagement in various types of communities and tools that are useful to become proficient in community work.
> » Managers want to encourage or support their staff's community involvement. If staff are hesitant to enter that world, managers can use some of the tips in this book to motivate them. Understanding motivation and building engagement are critical to successful communities, and managers will find some techniques that can be used for motivating teamwork in their own organizations.
> » Funders make many community projects possible. They can use the lessons from this book to help projects be more successful. As the technology world shifts, funders must be aware of changing realities about community sustainability, and not assume past solutions will continue to work.

Those who are working on starting up new communities will learn from the history of library technology and from established communities. They will have chances to try new things and avoid what were, in hindsight, obvious mistakes. They can avoid missed opportunities. I will go into more detail later about specific considerations for new communities, but in addition to everything else, it is important to pay special attention to choosing names for communities, determining appropriate legal structures, and creating a strong ethical framework for members.

■ Conclusion

Library technology communities are not perfect. No community is. Looking for what we can improve, retool, or rethink in a constantly shifting community landscape is a job that will never end. However, the history of library technology proves that this is a worthwhile pursuit. There is a long and vibrant history of cooperation both within and among organizations to create solutions. Starting with that history will set up the background for how communities work and review what types of communities are most prevalent today. Of course, every day there will be new ideas for new communities—in the months during which I was researching this book, I became involved with several incipient communities in library technology and related areas. By the time you read this, there will have been many more great ideas. That should not be discouraging but should tell us that this is work worth pursuing.

CHAPTER 2

A HISTORY OF COMMUNITY IN LIBRARY PROJECTS

Community is not new to libraries. Libraries would not exist without some sense of community, even if that community originally only extended to a religious order or scholarly enclave. Within the past 150 years (and the last 50 years for library technology), libraries and librarians have increasingly come together to form associations and other groups to further collaboration and resource sharing. New communities are always forming, but that does not make older communities irrelevant. Understanding why those older communities formed, the motivations of their members, and how those communities changed over time helps us to understand the present. User groups, too, have existed alongside library automation software from the beginning. The very act of automating libraries successfully required a strong community effort, and the consortiums that sprang up during that time still remain in some fashion or other, even as their focus has changed.

Although library technology has had a unique trajectory in certain areas, it generally has followed larger trends in the technology world. Library software has evolved from batch processes run on mainframes to software-as-a-service (SaaS) and cloud computing, just as in the rest of the world. Certain library communities are unique to the needs of libraries, but many communities owe their values and practices to the legacy of open source and free software communities in the larger world.

■ Associations and Consortiums

An association, for the purposes of this discussion, is a nonprofit organization incorporated for the purpose of educating, supporting, and setting standards for professionals. My focus will be primarily on the United States and its most influential organizations. This is not meant to ignore international bodies such as the International Federation of Library Associations (IFLA). International cooperation between libraries is vital for the success of community projects, and there will be several examples throughout the book of projects with connections among the United States and other countries. As well, much of the history of open source software culture is international.

For librarians in the United States, the American Library Association (ALA) has perhaps the greatest name recognition as a library association. Officially founded in 1876 and incorporated in 1879, it is the oldest community that we will consider in this book. The original intention of ALA was "to enable librarians to do their present work more easily and at less expense" (ALA 2008). Over the years, ALA's scope expanded beyond that pragmatic goal to efforts such as the promulgation of ethical guidelines for libraries and promotion of reading, especially among children. Today, it is a sprawling organization with niches for every type of librarianship and libraries. Given its breadth, coupled with its periodic organizational review initiatives, it may not be the ideal model for new projects to follow. Yet ALA's original idea of doing work "more easily" and with "less expense" remains an important motivating factor in technical projects in libraries, especially as shifting budgets and institutional mandates to update technology force us to do more with less—or, rather, to use technology to do more through automation.

Communities often experience tension in the balance between expertise and general knowledge. Associations tend to have a wider focus, so specializations may end up breaking off into their own organizations as their needs more widely diverge—and those break-off organizations may in turn become too specialized, which sends their members back to a more general organization.

Take the example of the Society of American Archivists (SAA), which formed in 1935 as an offshoot of the American Historical Association. The intention of SAA was to address the specialized needs of archivists, who, because of their own distinct professional identities and rules, were not receiving the attention they needed from the larger organization. Although the group was initially inclined to restrict membership exclusively to those employed in archives, it ultimately encompassed people with archival competency in general (Townsend 2013, 164–66). SAA, with its 6,200 members and some 45 sections, has itself become a complicated place. This illustrates aptly how specialized organizations can go on to become more general, and thus create smaller specialized offshoots.

For a similar set of reasons, library associations with a highly technical focus began appearing in the 1960s. These associations sought to address an increasing need for specialization in technical skills, while avoiding the strict membership limits or expertise requirements that were the norm in some groups. This was the reason for the founding of what eventually became the ALA division Library Information Technology Association (LITA).

The precursor to LITA was the Committee on Library Automation (COLA), which was formed in 1965 after a group got together in 1964 at the second Clinic on Library Applications of Data Processing at the University of Illinois Urbana-Champaign. One small group met at that clinic to discuss automated serials control systems and wanted to continue the discussion. Rather than trying to schedule meetings around clinics or institutes, which had restricted attendance and challenging schedules, the group decided to try to meet at more general conferences. COLA established an informal structure with minimal governance (Salmon 1967).

The problem with COLA was that it restricted membership to people who actively engaged in developing these systems. Few people at the time had much hands-on technical expertise, and they needed a place to have conversations and begin learning. An evening meeting at the 1965 ALA Annual Conference in Detroit included several hundred attendees who discussed the dire need for coordinated action for professional development in library automation. "It was pointed out that much of the current activity was badly planned, imperfectly executed, and unnecessarily expensive, simply because there was very little opportunity for librarians to exchange information with each other" (Salmon 1967, 638). In 1967, the new ALA Information Science and Automation Division (ISAD) had its first meeting in New York with hundreds of people in attendance.

Much of its initial work was to establish a journal and conferences where papers could be distributed. Over the following years, ISAD established several regional institutes, preconferences, and clinics to allow librarians who could not attend national meetings to learn more about library automation. In 1977, ISAD changed its name to the Library Information Technology Association (LITA). Some fifty years after the founding of LITA, the boards of several ALA divisions entered talks to merge, as finances became tighter and technology was prevalent throughout libraries rather than confined to individual departments. The internet has changed the problems of information sharing—rather than a lack of information, there is more than people can keep up with. Technology is far more accessible, and facility with technology is a basic job requirement. The conundrum remains, however, of needing knowledge and skills yet lacking enough knowledge to join a specialized community.

Consortiums can fill a similar role to associations, particularly in filling gaps in technical expertise at individual libraries. Consortiums are groups of libraries that join together to meet a common purpose, usually resource sharing, technology training, or technical infrastructure. The consortial model is a popular one for maintaining technical projects long-term, but as we will see, consortiums must adapt to changing technical circumstances in the same manner as associations.

Associations and consortiums can provide some lessons to technical communities, especially around governance options. Some community projects have a traditional association model, with an executive director, elected board of directors, and membership dues that give members voting rights. Others have a more informal model with leadership by consensus but may need to monitor shifting governance methods as community needs change.

Associations face challenges with declining membership. The instinct to limit membership to a narrowly defined set of experts is tempting because it may seem to increase efficiency. This is a risky proposition, however, because this inherently limits the scope of what the organization can do, and risks failure when those experts move on. On the other side, all projects should start with a manageable scope, and expanding the scope may be frustrating to current members as missions change.

Although this is true of all projects, the realities of the history of library technology make it particularly true. Libraries have staffs of varying sizes and technical ability. Their access to disparate technology frameworks differs, as does the ability to make their own technology decisions outside of a larger entity such as a city or university. Throughout time, libraries have had to work together and make their own needs mesh with others, and deal with all the compromise and frustration that can entail.

■ History of Technical Projects in Libraries

Automation in libraries always has been about sharing, even before it was possible to e-mail colleagues or download open source software. In the 1930s, well before the introduction of anything like modern computers, library automation began with Hollerith punched cards. Ralph Parker's experiments with these at the University of Texas were so inspirational to Frederick Kilgour that he adapted them at Harvard, and eventually transitioned to McBee Keysort cards (Kilgour 1987, 381). Parker and Kilgour had never met, proving that library technology can be shared and improved upon over distributed networks, even ones that must operate by telephone and mail.

Library automation began in earnest in the 1960s. The push for automation was helped along more by practical realities than by idealism, though that too was present. First, there was a massive increase in college enrollment at that time: 41 percent of recent high school graduates were enrolled in college in 1960, which jumped to 51 percent by 1965. Although percentages leveled off, the actual number of enrollees was much higher due to the larger youth population (National Center for Education Statistics 2007). Second, in order to see the efficiencies that automation promised, shared cataloging and standards would be necessary. The MARC standard began development at the Library of Congress in 1966 and started to be more widely adopted by the late 1960s and early 1970s (Avram 1968, 2).

Another point about increased efficiency and shared cataloging was a complicating factor, as the realities of technology at this time meant that any automation software had to work on whatever system the campus or city had, because in many cases libraries would have to rent time on computers to run their programs. Few libraries had the infrastructure to support automation at any high level, and only a few research libraries were realistically able to create their own automated library systems.

The juncture of practical requirements to complete a greater volume of work quickly and more idealistic ideas about sharing catalog records led to the contrasting attitudes that prevailed during this time. Some expected that libraries could only automate—or even continue to exist—by joining together. Others felt that taking an independent route to automation was not only possible for each library, but preferable. The question whether to collaborate or go it alone has not changed, certainly, but in the late 1960s one particularly successful communal project made collaboration an appealing prospect for many libraries.

That project was OCLC (originally the Ohio College Library Center). The philosophy behind OCLC brings us back to Frederick Kilgour and his punched cards at Harvard. Eventually Kilgour moved to the Yale Medical Library and used similar methods to streamline the collections there. In 1961 he first began to work seriously on computerization in libraries and joined forces with the Harvard and Columbia medical libraries. This project lasted until 1966, resulting in its notable product, a "Selected List of Acquisitions," which cut the time to prepare a new book list from one week to one hour. The project ended when Harvard left the collaboration in June 1966, and though Yale was able to continue with computerized card creation, Kilgour later reflected, "I learned from it to never again become involved in a cooperative project having only a few contributing participants" (Kilgour 1987, 383).

He held this opinion throughout the rest of his career. In 1965, he finally met Ralph Parker in person when the Committee of Librarians of the Ohio College Association (OCA) hired Kilgour and Parker as consultants. Their task was to determine what model made the most sense for a new shared bibliographic center for Ohio college libraries. Rather than go with a traditional bibliographic center, they determined that a "computerized, online, shared cataloging system" would be best, because it would "automatically create an online union catalog" (Kilgour 1987, 383). This was the genesis for what would eventually become OCLC. Because OCLC had the first successful shared cataloging system, it was attractive to other libraries, which saw it as the only practical way to automate their libraries and improve access to materials.

The centralization and cooperation of libraries was, to Kilgour and Parker, an inevitable progression. In 1967, Parker envisioned technology to mean the destruction of the small library—he saw automation as a force that would necessarily end the small operation. Just as the rise of the supermarket had changed the expectations for what type and amount of food should be available, the standards for access to materials from libraries and schools would rise. Libraries would grow, combine, and cooperate to meet these needs, and eventually computerization would lead to a national communication system of bibliographic networks that would benefit small libraries. Yet, as he wrote at the time, "At least another decade will be required before individual libraries can be partners in a broad, comprehensive, educational communications network by means of typewriter keyboards and television screens" (Parker 1967, 671). Although the introduction of monitor screens for personal computers was indeed some way off, OCLC started its cooperative catalog just a few years later, which led to the formation of state and regional networks for the use of mainframe computers that were not available in individual libraries.

For any of this cooperation to work, libraries had to agree to machine-readable standards for creating bibliographic records. The most important standards development of the time was MARC, the pilot project that was led by Henriette Avram of the Library of Congress and which was sponsored by the Council on Library and Information Resources (CLIR). In her final report on the project outcome, Avram wrote, "Libraries are on the brink of automation. It is to be hoped that the computer can be exploited as a tool in libraries so that they can better solve the needs of scholarship, science, and technology. MARC is a first step in this direction" (Avram 1968, 1). Work began on MARC in 1965 following an initial study in 1964, and the pilot project began in 1966. Sixteen libraries participated in the project, chosen using a selection process that aimed to distribute participant types of libraries, geographical locations, numbers of personnel, and funding availability. The libraries included several large public and private academic research libraries and several specialized science research laboratory libraries, as well as the Montgomery County Public Schools in Rockville, MD, and the Nassau County Library System on Long Island (Avram 1968, 4–5).

By May 1968, the pilot project had produced over 40,000 machine-readable titles. Avram noted that "the concept of sharing information via networks preceded MARC, but MARC has accelerated the planning and implementation," and listed a number of networks working on computerized technical processing centers (Avram 1968, 83). MARC had made it more economical to centralize bibliographic record creation, but what it did not solve was the question of a whether a library system could manage operations. The dream of an integrated library system (ILS) that would reuse data for purchasing, inventory management, and circulation was a widespread topic of discussion in the 1960s. Building such a system, however, was a complex undertaking. For libraries with the desire and the resources, it was an exhilarating challenge.

Ironically, NOTIS, the library system that was one of the exemplars in the literature of that time that addressed the attempt to develop a system by a library itself, ended up being one of the best early examples of cooperation among units in an organization, and ultimately the wider library community. Northwestern University Libraries started developing the system in the mid-1960s. The impetus was a new library building, and the project was led collaboratively by Velma Veneziano, a systems analyst at the Northwestern University Library, and James Aagaard, an associate professor of computer sciences and electrical engineering at Northwestern University (Aagaard 1987). In a 1976 article, Veneziano and Aagaard discussed whether it made financial sense for a library to attempt to build its own system. They felt the answer tended more toward "yes" than "no," in their own case, but this was primarily because they had approached the problem more realistically than other libraries by staffing the project with a small group of people with the appropriate expertise (Veneziano and Aagaard 1976). The appropriate expertise was not all within the library, however, nor would it remain at Northwestern.

In the late 1970s and early 1980s, NOTIS became a community project with the first installation at other institutions. NOTIS user groups started meeting in 1983. Northwestern found that it was not practical or desirable to support the project because of a broadening customer base within the library. This eventually led to it becoming a separate company in the late 1980s, which was acquired by Ameritech in 1991. NOTIS remained in use by Northwestern until 1998, at which point it switched to Voyager. The last institution stopped using NOTIS in 2012. The NOTIS user group continued until 1998 and provided an important avenue for support throughout (Specht 2017).

Other large research libraries found that partnerships between developers from a commercial background and librarians were essential to their automation projects. In 1968, Richard Johnson described how the Stanford library worked with its IBM development partner and the university computing center to create a printed book catalog produced by computer (which was determined to be cheaper than a card catalog). He wrote that "through a program of mutual education, the librarian learned of the computer and what it could do and what it could not do; and systems and computer personnel learned of the library's requirements and desires" (Johnson 1968, 15). That ability to find a shared understanding and learning to speak a common language remains the essence of successful collaborations.

The Stanford library's creation of a printed catalog at $32 per hour of machine time ended up costing between $25,000 to $30,000 a year, or around $180,000 in today's dollars. It determined that future developments for "on-line consultation" (not online in the sense of the internet, but in real-time on a terminal) would be more convenient, but ultimately deemed the project a success for the following reasons: it was able to do the work in-house, had a good relationship with IBM, a positive working attitude in the library, no problems getting time on the computer, adequate funding, and enough time to complete the work on schedule.

A convergence of these factors in Stanford's favor indicates why not many other libraries were able to replicate its success, which depended heavily on an institutional prioritization of technology. The *idea* of sharing is important even when the specifics of sharing software may be complicated. The ideological aims of cooperative projects may favor a community-based development model that is unrealistic for an individual library to continue supporting unless that is a special priority for that library.

■ Open Source, Free, or Commercial Software in Libraries

Stanford's experience was unusual at the time but illustrates a fact that is still true today: large research libraries are often able to go off and build their own solutions. The difference today is that large research libraries are more likely to incorporate open source software into their approaches rather than building a bespoke system from scratch. Here we must consider various models for support and distribution of software, which are relevant to library technology precisely because of their ideological differences. Why would someone create software for free? And, if you were setting out to create a new tool for libraries, why would you consider creating a tool developed and supported by a community rather than a commercial product?

The reality of open source software in the current library technology software was by no means inevitable, but earlier collaborations among libraries to develop MARC and improve automation made it more likely that libraries would share successful solutions with each other. Understanding the cultural differences between commercial, free, and open source software provides some context for why a certain project would end up following a certain model, and what type of community could exist around a project.

Drawing too sharp a distinction among software types would be simplistic, but in general the differences are around the way in which the source code is made available. Commercial software (e.g., Microsoft Windows), has proprietary source code that the end user cannot change, and is purchased from a company. Much of the web exists on closed source software that is free to use, which is not the same as free or open source software. "Free" can mean no-cost (usually termed *gratis*), or it can mean free to modify and copy (*libre*). Free software comes out of a tradition of people working for free on software, which led to a desire for permissive reuse licenses (Barron 2013, 601). The Free Software Foundation (2018) maintains the GNU Public License and its derivatives, as well as a list of compatible licenses that make software "free"; according to its philosophy, users must have the ability to run a program for any purpose, see the source code, distribute copies, and distribute modified copies. "Non-free" open source software may only meet a few of these categories, but still be developed by a distributed network and available at no cost. For the purposes of this book, I will use "open source" to refer to the range of licenses and approaches that developers take. However, it is important to recognize the differences in ideology, particularly when considering whether to join a community. Projects with a strong emphasis on free software philosophies usually emphasize this fact in documentation because it is so important to the community norms.

Community is about more than the specific approaches and intentions of a project, especially in the legal sense. The current landscape of library software runs from completely free and open software with specific free software licenses to hosted and proprietary tools. Practically speaking, however, software distribution licenses have little to do with the aims or norms of a community. For libraries with appropriate infrastructure and staff, it is possible to develop software locally and choose a model for sustainability, or to customize open source projects for their own purposes. For many libraries, however, it is not feasible to choose open source solutions, no matter how much they might wish to because of cultural or ideological points of view. Infrastructure provided by a city or a university may restrict choices for what can be installed, and libraries may lack staff who can contribute enough time to open source communities. These realities do not mean that these libraries cannot participate in community, however, as we will see.

The exemplar of open source development, for better or worse, is the Linux operating system, described as a "bazaar" style of development by Eric Raymond in his influential book of essays *The Cathedral and the Bazaar* (1999). The development of Linux was a public and messy process, with the best offerings for each piece of the software winning out. Raymond contrasts this with what he characterizes as the reverent, quiet, and contained development of earlier tools like Emacs (a text editor). The challenge for all software development is that the best models for designing software and for bringing a product to market do not always align. Frederick Brooks describes these issues in *The Design of Design* (2010), in which he demonstrates that what may work best in design as a practice does not always have the greatest commercial strength or best alignment with current technical realities. The practices that developers follow and the methods they use are not necessarily in accordance with commercial practices, or what is in the best interest of users. Brooks admitted that although he did not have much direct experience with open source development, he thought it was an excellent model, provided that the work was done by people who understood the problems to be solved and were themselves the users of the product (Brooks 2010, 57).

No matter what the development model is, popular and widely used products can become victims of their own success. As projects move away from the original creators, the user-builders are further distanced from the product. Hence, the product's design and features become bloated as developers attempt to meet more and more use cases at a remove. Once the software reaches a certain complexity, the user community may spend all its time understanding the software but lack any actual ability to improve it. An open source development model does not necessarily help in this situation. Library technology and its associated communities provide many examples. Downfalls in commercial software are, at least in hindsight, seen as occurring when companies became too greedy. Open source projects can become impossible to support properly by any but the largest institutions once too many dependencies have been introduced.

The earliest integrated library systems were either developed by vendors or by institutions. As we have seen, when libraries were able to find good partnerships with others in their institutions or with other institutions, they were often able to build something that could be successfully implemented. Even in the case of a commercial product, the level of connection between the vendor and the institution was much stronger. Geac (an early commercial ILS) consultants spent weeks in the field installing computers and software at library sites and training the staff. The connection between developer and library was stronger in these cases. Over time, however, this started to shift. Geac was always a niche product, but eventually a desire to capture more of the market led to less specialization and less clear focus on the future of the company (Syed 2011, 114).

NOTIS (the Northwestern-developed library system) provides an example of a library-developed platform that was eventually spun off into a commercial product rather than being maintained by the community. Velma Veneziano described the problem in a 1993 speech at the NOTIS Users Group, "Wouldn't it be nice, they reasoned, to be able to partly finance the development of the features we needed at Northwestern by the sale of the system to other libraries. To make a long story short, we eventually yielded to temptation and set up a marketing operation in the library, which for reasons I won't go into, proved disastrous" (Specht 2014). The culture at Northwestern made a commercial avenue for NOTIS the sustainable solution choice, but despite Veneziano's opinion, the community-oriented nature of the development meant that a strong community survived commercialization.

It is now easier to build a hosting and consulting business around a tool while still maintaining a community focus. One example is LibraryH3lp, which was originally a consortial chat product designed for universities in North Carolina, but eventually spun off into a hosted commercial product used by hundreds of libraries. The advantage of this type of product is that the community focus is there from the beginning, and maintaining that focus is a priority of the developers and maintainers of the product (Sessoms and Sessoms 2008).

The idea of building a hosting and consulting business around open source software is an avenue for sustainability but can cause tension around ideological takes on open source. Koha is a hugely popular open source ILS that was originally developed by the Horowhenua Library Trust in

New Zealand in 1999 to address Y2K issues. Several consulting companies provided support to libraries wishing to install and maintain Koha. One of these companies was LibLime, which in 2009 created a new hosted version of Koha that many felt violated the spirit of open source development, because it "forked" (that is, created a new version whose changes would never be integrated with the main branch of development) the original project (Ransom 2009). LibLime was acquired in 2011 by PTFS, another company that had also provided support for Koha. As part of this acquisition, PTFS obtained ownership of a number of pieces of intellectual property associated with Koha, including the US trademark of the name (Ojala 2010). Luckily, this did not spell the end for the original version of Koha, which in late 2018 was up to version 18, with several active contributors and an active community with good supports built in.

Controversies around support companies have not necessarily ended. A recent example is Virginia Tech's decision to adopt Koha and contract ByWater Solutions for hosting and development support. An associate dean at Virginia Tech, Michael Kucsak, stated that one of the reasons was that ByWater's support would cost less than it would to hire a systems administrator (Enis 2018). This is a good thing for the Koha community, of course, who will benefit from any enhancements that ByWater creates for Virginia Tech, but it shifts the locus of control. This decision points to the challenges in engaging with open source communities and choosing open source software even for well-resourced institutions.

■ Conclusion

Open source software developed by a community ought to be inherently community-focused. The more complicated question is how to ensure the software and its community is maintained over time. Eric Raymond argued strongly for open source development supported by companies, which can make economic arguments for doing do. Cost sharing by hiring and supporting developers in open source communities means that users of the software get to take advantage of a better-quality product at a lower price—and actively participating rather than merely using means that the users get a say in the direction taken. Making software open source spreads risk around and ensures that access to important software does not depend on retaining a specific developer (Raymond 1999, 156–8). As well, anything developed and kept in-house needs to be maintained in-house. Making a tool open means that the entire developer community, a resource with far more expertise than any one organization could offer, can help maintain it. In future chapters we will see many examples of open source software communities in libraries, and the many ways that they have found sustainability over time.

Technology communities can exist without technical infrastructure. Social media is supposed to be entirely about building community. By design, it is free and easy to use because the platforms want to draw users to attract advertisers. Creating a community around such a platform has a low barrier to entry. Yet the tradeoff of relying on a commercial platform is that the community has no say over the future of the software, even if they can dictate their own cultural norms within the group. Where to draw the line between relying on social media or other platforms and where to focus on building infrastructure for control are not questions with an easy answer, though in later chapters we will see some examples of tools that can help with this.

We cannot rely on a simple definition of community technology projects in libraries, even as many of them are rooted in historical realities of software development. Some library communities look like open source software communities. Some look like user groups formed to support commercial software. Some are based on associations. Consideration of past practices helps us take the best from the past to create new types of communities. No matter the type of community or its historical roots, there are practices that are more likely to lead to successful communities.

CHAPTER 3

COMMUNITY BEST PRACTICES

L ibrary technology is ever-changing, as is technology of all kinds. But building community is not about the technology. It is about the people who make up that community. Working with them is, in most ways, more challenging than any technical problem. Success comes from building psychologically healthy communities and using tools and techniques intentionally to achieve this. Being intentional is important for creating inclusive communities. Often groups will form organically in structures that end up being exclusive because the initial set of discussions or the push to accomplish work will draw from the same pool of people. Some potential participants may have a strong desire to learn new technical skills or participate in a complex discussion, but lack the confidence to do so, even when they possess many other useful attributes (e.g., strong writing ability, project management, or other "softer" skills).

Looking at how communities have shaped themselves traditionally in open source development will help us understand how similar patterns have emerged in library technology communities. Much of the current landscape of community in library technology grows out of open source software, and the history of that movement is evident in the ways communities operate and communicate. For example, the Samvera Community has adapted some of the Apache Software Foundation principles known as

"The Apache Way" for its code and community governance—"The Samvera Way" includes methods such as transparent voting and public documentation (Branan 2017).

Understanding the motivations of technology community members helps to explain how these communities succeed. Some of this has to do with motivations for why people participate in open source development, but beyond that, there is a rich literature in business psychology and nonprofit management on motivation among volunteers. Using all this background helps us to understand how to plan a community more deliberately and how to motivate members—usually volunteers—to stay engaged with the work.

■ The Hacker Ideology: Its Uses and Abuses

The hacker ideology is a mindset that open source communities both attract and inculcate, and which drives much of the development in library technology. Although this is not the only motivating factor for library communities, it is one that, in my experience, prevails. When outsiders talk about hackers in library technology, they may be thinking of the types of people who grab library proxy server logins and post pay-walled academic journal articles online. This is not the "hacker ideology" about which Eric Raymond writes in his book *The Cathedral and the Bazaar* (1999), in which he describes the traditional use of the term "hacker" as someone who likes to learn and build her own systems, not someone who is trying to break into others' systems. As with many ideologies, it can be used for good and ill. Understanding this helps us to understand why library technology can work well, and how it can be exclusionary or downright toxic.

Open source developers, or hackers in this case, operate in a gift economy, where recognition of expertise is a critical motivation for participation on the individual level. Finding the best contributors for these communities relies on motivating talented people to do work for free. Unlike the exchange economy that underlies most work arrangements, hackers exist in an "abundance economy." Abundance means that your reputation is increased by what you give away, rather than what you keep. But managing reputations in this economy is a balancing act. *You* cannot call *yourself* a hacker. This is something that must be recognized from within the community, which means that one should never brag about individual achievements to try to gain status. By the same token, a fundamental principle of open source development is to never remove someone's name as a participant. The motivation to participate is about building a reputation, and by removing the name of contributors and thus denying them credit, you remove the motivation.

The best "bazaar" style development is about people solving problems that they find personally important, "scratching your own itch," as the saying goes. Development starts when a developer tries to solve a problem she is experiencing. Eric Raymond's example from his own work is an e-mail client, but many librarians need to develop applications to handle issues such as open hours calendars on websites, research guides, and statistics tracking. Individuals may start working on solving a problem, share their solutions with a community, and see if anyone else is interested in working on the problem as well.

Other rules for open source development that come out of the hacker ideology: reuse code and solutions where possible, treat users like co-developers, hand off the work carefully when you are no longer able to work on it, listen to the good ideas of others, and be willing to admit when you are wrong. In many ways, this is about respect—for the problems, for the work that has come before you, and most importantly for the users and co-developers. Such practices are not easy to follow, however, and as the "bazaar" idea indicates, a certain messiness and churn is to be expected. In looking back at ten years of conference presentations, I found some projects half-finished and abandoned, and some projects that still work but whose developers have moved on. The reasons for this are many—we will look at some specific factors later—but being a hacker requires the ability to be comfortable with a level of uncertainty.

The cultural practices of hackers motivate certain people to do great work. But even if the idea is alluring, the actual practices may be off-putting. Within library technology and the larger technology culture it has become clear that hacker ethics are not inclusive. This is partly by design—the idea is that only certain people can be included in an inner circle, which they can join only after years of toil, which leads to a senior group of decision-makers, which requires that communities have some exclusivity. Beyond that, looking at the unstated preferences of a culture illuminates some values that may only be evident to excluded groups. Raymond's work itself is an illustration of this. His observations are critical to understanding how the culture of community technology works, but the fact that in over 200 pages the only pronoun used is "he" and an example of a contributor role is "Lord High Fixer" speaks for itself.

It is hard to criticize Raymond now because he was accurate in describing how the hacker culture of the time operated. Unfortunately, while that work dates to the 1990s, things have not changed all that much in the last twenty years. Even in 2017, a survey of GitHub users found that 95 percent of respondents identified as men. The hacker ideology and open source traditions are not sacrosanct, and modern technology communities should not hesitate to abandon many aspects of them. Even though there were always women in computer science, and librarians like Henriette Avram were instrumental in creating modern library technology, women in library technology still do not always feel comfortable in what were traditionally male-dominated spaces of open source.

This sense of discomfort is not unique to library technology or open source. When Margolis and Fisher worked with women studying computer science at Carnegie Mellon University in the 1990s, they looked at reasons that women drop out of computer science programs. Factors such as "geek culture" and assumptions about what a "real" programmer looks like lead to discomfort in spaces where computer culture dominates to the exclusion of all else (Margolis and Fisher 2002, 68). Women in male-dominated fields across all disciplines rate their skill level as lower, even when their grades are equivalent to men's (82). Women perceive themselves as less able to do technical work, and a lack of confidence in their abilities leads to a lack of interest as they avoid the work, which (in turn) creates a vicious cycle that increases their lack of confidence (86–87).

After Chris Bourg gave a keynote at the 2018 Code4Lib conference that suggested, among other things, that outward signals of geek culture be removed from workplaces to make them more inclusive, she was harassed by people online. Certainly, she is not the first woman to be harassed online by men for suggesting systemic changes to improve inclusion in technology. This harassment brought issues in library technology into wider focus, however, and made it clear that our space is not immune to such behavior. A problem with the hacker ideology and prestige motivations, and a major factor that can dissuade potential contributors to open source projects, are the enforcement mechanisms, which include flaming (i.e., online harassment) and shunning (i.e., exclusion). Raymond states that ideally these techniques are the last resort in governing an open source community

(Raymond 1999, 128). For too many on social media, however, these are the first and last techniques for maintaining the status quo.

Creating social cohesion and sense of camaraderie in any technical environment without being exclusionary is an ongoing challenge. Christopher Syed, biographer of the Geac integrated library system, describes the scene at Geac in the 1980s as one similar to technology companies today, with a focus on geek culture, game-playing, no dress code, and individual developer control of schedules. This was a way of compensating creative people in nonmonetary ways, of course, but it also helped to create stronger teams in a company that required considerable work from its employees (Syed 2011, 60–61). But this, like other approaches, makes it challenging for people with more complicated lives or different interests to be integrated into the community.

Another example of a potentially problematic practice often used for building community is the idea of a "hackathon," or a focused period of time to work on technical problems. Hackathons started in the late 1990s and became an increasingly popular activity in library technology circles over the course of the first decade of the 2000s, starting with the Access Conference (a Canadian library technology conference) in 2002. Various organizations such as OCLC and the Digital Public Library of America have sponsored hackathons, and libraries themselves host hackathons, whether related to libraries or not, in their spaces. (Heller 2012a).

Although hackathons can create strong camaraderie and help coalesce a community around software, the stereotypical version is a group of people—usually young men—sitting around in an uncomfortable space, eating junk food, and not sleeping. Many people's schedules make it impossible to participate in such an event, even if it was not off-putting on its face. The word "hackathon" itself can be a problem because it implies competition in male-dominated culture. Communities or libraries should not refrain from holding such events but should be mindful that without a diverse group of planners, they will end up excluding people and probably will not produce a high-quality outcome (Lin 2016). Simple fixes like not using the word "hackathon" for social coding events, ensuring frequent breaks, healthy food and sleep, and deemphasizing competition in favor of collaboration are ways that communities can benefit from hackathon techniques.

Creating avenues for support for marginalized groups helps them stay involved in technology. Margolis and Fisher found that at Carnegie Mellon, one of the most important factors in retaining women in computer science was respect and support by teachers. Mentoring newer professionals is one way this can be applied in library technology. This research, which is mirrored by other studies with marginalized groups, found that it is crucial to have supportive learning communities and be surrounded by support networks of friends (103–4). Building such communities can be challenging without a critical mass of participants but creating safe spaces for mutual support should be a priority for communities looking to develop inclusive communities. Women in library technology have addressed this via collectives like LibTechWomen (which was founded in 2014). The research shows us that these types of communities-within-a-community do work. Some specific methods to build emotional support will be explored later in this chapter.

Eric Raymond described the process of becoming a hacker as one of watchful waiting until one's work is noticed by the community, without much of an ability to rush the process. That model does not help extend communities in new ways or invite new voices. People with motivations suited to that style of community may find engagement, but others will find the process slow, confusing, or uninteresting. Experienced members of the community should encourage newer or more peripheral members of community to speak up when they cannot understand why a community is making a certain choice. Responding to all questions with "read the manual" presupposes that it should be obvious there is a manual somewhere. If the community does not make something clear, then the correct response is to fix that problem rather than blaming others.

■ Motivating Strong Communities

Strong communities require committed participants, who are in most cases volunteers. Business psychology research that tries to understand why people volunteer suggests that determining this requires looking at the specific psychological motivations of volunteers. Much of this research is based on work done in the mid-1990s by a research team headed by Gil Clary and Mark Snyder. They developed a functional model of volunteer motivation called the Volunteer Functional Inventory (Clary et al. 1998). Functional, in this case, means that the same physical action can have different psychological motivations for different people. The model includes the following motivating factors:

» *Values.* Expressing altruistic feelings
» *Understanding.* Learning new skills that cannot be acquired elsewhere
» *Social.* Spending time with others
» *Career.* Believing that skills gained by volunteering will help with career aspirations
» *Protective.* Shielding the ego from negative self-perception or alleviating guilt about privilege
» *Enhancement.* Building on positive self-perceptions. (Clary et al. 1998, 1518)

This model is based on research on volunteer communities. Research results found that participants who had been motivated by achieving benefits from participation were happier and more inclined to volunteer long-term when they achieved the desired benefits (Clary et al. 1998, 1528). Other researchers have proposed additions or simplifications of Clary and Snyder's model. Some reduce the number of motivations, others add more. Regardless of if you are explicitly assessing motivations within this framework, you can glean some important information from it. People do work they are not being paid to do because something motivates them to do so. Knowing what those motivations are allows you to ensure that people are getting what they need and will stay committed.

For projects such as library communities that are based in the world of a profession, it is likely that motivations are career-focused, but also have a strong social and emotional component. For example, people participate in technology groups such as Code4Lib or LITA for the networking and social aspects just as much as to develop skills. Because time and professional development funds are limited, people may choose communities that have a stronger direct career focus, but still look for social elements, according to research LITA did about its own participants (Lee 2017). People who work in technology at libraries are more likely to work in small departments or are solo practitioners, which means they may be even more likely to seek out professional camaraderie in technology-related communities.

Indeed, the history of open source technology suggests that the social and emotional side of participation is important to recognize and nurture. The Free Software movement personified by Richard Stallman was, as Anne Barron suggests, "fueled by both an artistic and a social critique of capitalism" (Barron 2013, 610). Whether or not contributors to open source projects are explicitly making any political statement, it does seem that participation in such communities is motivated by a messiness, creativity, and joy that may not be present in other types of work.

Research supports this. Looking at participants in open source projects as a whole, motivations are often based on the perception that volunteer work will lead to more career opportunities. The 2017 GitHub Open Source Survey found that half of respondents thought that open source contribution was a factor in their current employment. By openly sharing code you have written, the thought goes, you will show potential employers what you can do, and they will be more likely to hire you. That perception may not be accurate, however. One study found that among German participants in open source software, 70 percent thought that this participation would be beneficial for their careers, when in fact it was not possible to identify any increase in wages. The researchers believe that participants' true motivations were values such as play, altruism, and respect of their peers. Although there are examples of open source participation leading to employment, that benefit seems to exist more within specific communities with well-established merit rankings (i.e., reputation), such as Apache (Bitzer, Geishecker, and Schröder 2017).

I once participated in a crowdsourcing transcription event where groups of people sat in a room together for an afternoon to transcribe newspapers. It was in concordance with a national event and had been widely promoted across my institution. Two distinct groups of participants attended: those who saw the fliers or social media posts and came out of interest, and those who for whom attendance was a class requirement. I later obtained access to the data from the participant survey and noticed something interesting. Although everyone got something out of the experience, nearly all the people who attended for fun wanted to do the work again, while only around 30 percent of the people who attended only because they had to fulfill a class requirement wanted to participate again. This anecdote is a reminder that fun is more of a motivator than obligation, certainly something that has proven true in open source communities.

By the same token, digital projects that rely on crowdsourcing should consider the ethics of attention. Grabbing people's attention through fun may get them to participate, but it creates a new form of unpaid labor. Attention is the new commodity, and app developers use addictive psychology or "ludic loops" to capture it. As Michael Harris notes, making use of the blank spaces in a person's life by harnessing their attention is not always a good thing, because it removes the opportunities for that person to do something else or simply enjoy quiet (M. Harris 2017, 66–67). The concept of "cognitive capitalism" is the recognition that using people's time and attention "via the social web… is pervasive and pernicious" (Perry and Beale 2015).

In Barron's analysis of free and open source software as critical social practice, she found that, ultimately, much of the character of open source culture has been remade into 1990s business leadership ideas of charismatic leaders and horizontal decision-making. In her estimation, all too often open source projects are just the same old capitalist enterprise, and the expectation of free labor has depressed wages, which has been ported over to the cultural sector at large. These critiques should not suggest that open source or crowdsourcing projects are always unethical, but that they have the potential to exploit the motivations of participants. Having a strong mission focus and a truly collaborative and creative spirit will make this less likely.

For people who would like to become involved in a community, but are not sure where to start, the concept of motivation can be helpful. Individuals can use the facets of motivation to determine goals for community involvement. For example, someone who identifies her primary motivation as wanting to learn more technical skills to enhance career prospects will find engagement with a development-focused community. Someone who has a values motivation may find a community that does outreach to underserved populations to be more engaging.

■ Understanding the Motivations of Your Community

People setting up a community may find it challenging to determine individual motivations. Furthermore, once understood, ensuring that the community meets those needs requires more effort than just hoping people will find the right place. In all projects that are successful, *community management* is critical. What this looks like differs by type of project, but without some person or group of people functioning in that role, problems will start to occur. The time to think about community management is before the community crystallizes.

The role of a community manager, whether officially appointed or someone who simply takes on the work, is to understand the community's motivations and needs. Community manager jobs are common at companies looking to build community in person and through social media or other online platforms. These positions might be called "Community Manager," "Engagement Manager," "Social Engagement Manager," or something similar. In library technology companies, this role can focus on developing the user community. For example, in spring 2018, OCLC advertised a Community Manager opening for someone to work on tasks including building community engagement, creating and sharing best practices, and identifying potential community leaders for collaboration.

Although some projects formally designate a community manager, in my own experience this tends to be an informal role that people with a strong interest in community building take on. An informal approach can work, but this has the potential to lead to burnout as people (often women) perform invisible emotional labor. And when people are too close to a community, it can be hard to see potential problems that are more obvious to outsiders or newer members. On the other hand, outsiders to a community cannot mandate changes they feel are necessary. Building mutual trust between these groups is necessary.

No matter who has the community manager role, understanding members requires knowing the community. Ideally, research should undergird community perceptions, using explicit measurement tools such as focus groups, surveys, or ethnographies. One useful tool for analyzing and communicating data about members with the community is personas, which are fictional profiles of "real" users. These are often used in product development but can be extremely helpful for understanding who wants to be involved in a community and use the tools created by the community, particularly during the early planning phases of a community or when it is time to begin strategic planning. Although personas, like any tool, can be misused, they can provide an opportunity to be empathetic with the community and tell a story about the data more meaningfully than a table of figures could ever do (Unger and Chandler 2009, 125).

Various library technology communities have used personas to understand their user communities to provide useful services to them. One example is HathiTrust, whose UX Advisory Group developed personas in 2011 to highlight its user types, which included scholars, teachers, students, and librarians. The LITA Personas Task Force developed a set of personas for LITA members in 2017, which were designed to define the members of the community to help enhance their experiences (Lee 2017).

Identified roles included librarians with general interests, library workers in technology, administrators, and committed community members. As all persona projects should, the group also created personas for nonmembers and tried to identify the reasons they were not participating in the community. These outsiders may be people who may not be aware of the community, or they may not realize that it would meet their needs—or perhaps would not meet their needs. Understanding what is out of scope for a community is useful.

Personas can be a helpful tool for developing engaged communities, especially when they are developed using a participatory design method that asks people about their own perceptions of their motivations. But it is important to test and question the information gathered this way to ensure that the people who feel uncomfortable stating their real motivations are not ignored. People may not feel comfortable sharing that their motivations for participating in a community are largely social if they want to work on the project during the work day, and people in a more social group may not feel comfortable stating their primary objective is to enhance their careers. Or, they may not realize that is a benefit for participating. Therefore, it is safer to assume that many kinds of motivations may be present, especially when dealing with a multicultural participant base. For example, volunteer research in communities with high religiosity found that religion may be a motivating factor for social reasons because religious institutions may set volunteering as a social norm (Butt et al. 2017).

An additional consideration is that people often feel pressured to do unpaid work on projects to gain experience for a future career. Pressure comes from both the open source world, where companies may hire people based on number of GitHub commits, and the library world, where people often do unpaid internships or practicums while in school. Crowdsourcing projects give the veneer of gamification to what is essentially unpaid digital labor. Although all these approaches have validity, they quickly become unethical without explicit discussion of the needs and true desires of the participants, and recognizing that people without the spare time to participate in these efforts will not be doing the work. Therefore, if understanding the motivations of the community has been based on who is doing unpaid labor, it is important to map out the ways in which others who want to participate but have been excluded can still be part of the community.

■ Maintaining Engagement

Once you understand the motivations of your community members, how do you keep them engaged with their work, especially given the challenges you will have identified for many of them? Management literature defines "engagement" in several ways, but it can be summarized as a state of being absorbed in one's work and a heightened sense of well-being that increases the likelihood that one will stay involved. Without long-term engagement, communities will start to dissipate, and the tools or projects that those communities developed may disappear.

The model for engagement proposed by Kerstin Alfes, Amanda Shantz, and Catherine Bailey is the most useful for library technology projects because it emphasizes both task support and emotion-oriented support (Alfes, Shantz, and Bailey 2016). Providing these types of support motivates volunteers to become immersed in their work. In more traditional volunteer work, an example of task support might include a recipe for preparing meals in a soup kitchen. For library technology, I categorize this as "getting unstuck technically," or the knowledge for how to work the technology. Emotional support for more traditional volunteer work might be ideas for engaging with homeless patrons of a soup kitchen. In the case of library technology, it might be "getting unstuck politically or socially" by introducing a tool to your colleagues or getting involved with the community. Both supports are essential. People must be able to use the tool, of course, but equally important is communicating about its use. One is hard without the other.

Library technology projects offer task and emotional support using a variety of methods. Based on the projects I looked at in researching this book, table 3.1 shows the types of support that successful projects offered for various phases of the work or to answer questions that people might have. Having multiple methods for support will help people throughout their involvement, from the most basic procedural questions to questions of culture and governance.

Not all the elements listed above need to be in place at the beginning of the project, but projects that are to be successful must at some point be explicit about how support happens and be willing to adjust as the needs of the community change. For example, a project may start with technical development calls, but as the non-developer community grows, additional opportunities for decision-making that are more about user

TABLE 3.1

TYPES OF EMOTIONAL AND TASK SUPPORT

	Task Support	Emotional Support
What is happening with the project	Detailed documentation and/or a wiki	Blog with news about the project
Cultural expectations	Open code on GitHub or another repository	Social media channels or other forums
Cultural expectations	Clear expectations for process	Code of conduct
Ability to have conversations	Technical mailing list or chat/Slack	General mailing list/ Slack
Decision-making opportunities	Technical development calls or meetings	User groups or conferences

needs or governance may be offered separately from the developer calls. Managing all these avenues for support is a significant amount of work and will take conscious effort to regularly review the state of the community and its changing needs. Has what was a purely social group moved to developing tools based on discussions by the members? Then it is time to make sure the task support offered is up-to-date.

■ Conclusion: Respect for Participants

Respect for people and their needs requires recognition of the human cost of technology. The "magic" of technology is prone to make us forget that physical infrastructure and human effort lie behind it. Stacie Williams has demonstrated that the physical and human infrastructure that makes digital information possible is demonstrably harmful to the environment. Digital media creates e-waste that cannot be disposed of ethically without care and attention, and the data centers that hold digital collections use land, fuel, and water. Collecting vast amounts of digital information is harmful, even when its existence contributes to research that could improve lives (Williams 2017). No digital project should be taken on blithely without acknowledging that there are no human costs of the work.

The people that digitize vast collections such as the Google Books project are made purposefully invisible, even as their hands are sometimes visible in the scanned images. This is a centuries-old practice known as "The Mechanical Turk," in which a trick is performed by a person hiding in a machine. The Mechanical Turk is also the name of an Amazon service that provides the services of human laborers needed to make the digital economy function. Low-paying and insecure jobs mean that workers, often women, are subject to exploitation. "Women provide the behind the scenes labor that is mystified as the work of computers, unglamorous work transformed into apparent algorithmic perfection" (Wen 2014). As automation increases, more people will fall into this status, and we must ensure that library technology communities maintain a strong ethical framework to alleviate injustice.

What should that ethical framework include? Whereas in the past "hacker ethics" were the primary form of ethics in community technology, a better model for the future might be the "ethics of care." Like hacker ethics, this assumes a community is working together for success. The ethics of care, as originally described by Nel Noddings, is not a set of rules for behavior, nor a purely arbitrary set of actions, but an ethic that "recognizes and calls forth human judgement across a wide range of fact and feeling, and [which] allows for situations and conditions in which judgement (in the impersonal, logical sense) may be properly put aside in favor of faith and commitment" (Noddings 1984, 25). Tara Robertson provides the seminal example of this in her discussion of the digitization of *On Our Backs*, a lesbian pornography magazine. When Robertson discovered that the magazine was going to be digitized, she was originally excited about increasing access to the publication. Then she realized that this could potentially be harmful for the people who had appeared in the magazine but had not given consent for this type of distribution; in fact, this type of distribution was not even possible when the magazine was originally published. As she discovered, several people she spoke to specifically did not give consent and found the digitization hurtful. Librarians may think of digitization as always being a positive benefit, but in this case the community that provided the collection was actively harmed by the digitization. Ultimately the company that digitized the magazine removed it (albeit for unrelated reasons) and claimed it would try to follow better ethical practices in the future.

Keeping the needs and intentions of a community in mind from the beginning is important in cultural heritage digitization projects as well as in any community-oriented project. Robertson gives an example of an approach that was more thoughtful from its start. When the New Zealand Electronic Text Collection wanted to digitize a book on Maori tattooing, it did so only after consulting with the Maori community about what would be appropriate and then wrote a report laying out the options considered and the eventual choices. A similar effort has resulted in "TK Labels," which allow indigenous communities to explicitly assign usage rights to cultural material that is not under copyright (Robertson 2016). Social media is another area of concern, because it includes a huge amount of information people shared in public without the expectation of it being used in other contexts or remixed in ways that could be damaging to them. The Documenting the Now project is creating a set of principles and tools for the ethical collection of social media data for research.

Such examples indicate not only the type of ethics needed for work on digital projects, but also how to treat members of the community doing the work. Understanding the types of people who are interested in trying to get involved will help community managers to shape the perception of what the community can offer. Shaping perception is not about lying to people about what the community aims to do, but rather demystifying the paths to engagement.

CHAPTER 4

THE COMMUNITY LANDSCAPE IN LIBRARY TECHNOLOGY

M any projects have as a stated goal the desire to create or support a community. This chapter will break the landscape down into four specific types: *general technology associations* or *consortiums, user groups, small-scale distributed development*, and *large-scale projects*. Each type of project may incorporate aspects from other types, but they are worth considering separately. Specific types of communities need different approaches to management, from planning the scope to choosing appropriate task and emotional supports. People interested in joining these communities likewise will find different potential avenues for engagement. Within the landscape of projects, each type of community has its own origins in the history of library technology and unique features. Each has its own trends and examples of what success looks like. Each project structure has benefits and challenges. And each project has different opportunities for engagement.

■ Paying for a Growing Project

We have already established that defining the values of a community and making the community work for the participants are major challenges no matter the type of community. Another general challenge—and one that is particularly acute for library projects with short-term funding—is financial sustainability. We also know from the history of open source software and library technology that economic arguments are part of deciding whether going with a community or a commercial model makes more sense. In addition, examples such as the New Media Consortium bankruptcy show that even apparently successful projects can be suffering economically. Therefore, before looking at the specific community types, we will consider some economics of library technology communities in general.

Scholarly infrastructure projects are, according to Cameron Neylon, a kind of "collective good," which is something that benefits many, but does not necessarily have a clear path for funding or maintenance. To succeed, these projects require a committed set of participants who are willing to fund and support them long-term. The problems with scholarly infrastructure (which describes most library technology projects) occur in trying to move these projects from smaller, grant-funded projects to larger, subscription or consortially funded projects. Grant funding creates a clear set of participants and deliverables, and gives the people working on a project time to create something of sufficient use and value that others will want to use. This works well up to a point, but as Neylon describes, using collective action to create something that is a collective good becomes challenging as the size of a community increases. Trying to get hundreds of disparate users or institutions to agree on a path forward is necessarily harder than with a small project team, even if they have been using participatory design techniques. And there will always be political problems and distress in communities over artificial barriers to access for digital goods (Neylon 2017, 2).

Putting up a pay wall of any kind is always unpopular, and in Neylon's analysis there are three ways to avoid this as projects move from small to large, self-sustaining communities. The first is compulsion, for example, a required union fee or indirect cost budget slices that institutions tend to rely on. The second is a by-product of some other service, which means creating an entity like CrossRef to register DOIs. Publishers must pay to join, but the by-product of DOIs (which is the service publishers pay for) is a collective benefit. The third is oligopoly, which is usually something created by funders in the research sphere that forces a collective action (e.g., PubMed Central) where people are required to make their work open access as a condition of funding (Neylon 2017, 3). The latter two scenarios are often held up as possible avenues to help community projects become sustainable, but there is no guarantee that a collective good produced by any community is compelling enough to get others to join.

Neylon gives case studies for several approaches in the scientific research sphere that mirror approaches taken by library community projects. Cambridge Crystallographic Data Centre offers free access to datasets, but requires a subscription for additional services, which created a collective good of central data. This model struggles when there is more pressure for access. The commercial side of access provides revenue, but there are potential opportunity costs. There could be non-collective benefits for services other than data, or consortium funding by industry and public that rely on this. Another approach is taken by the Arabidopsis Information Resource, which originally was funded publicly; when that funding ended, it moved to a subscription model for heavy users with higher corporate rates. The community that relies on this data is small, but willing to pay for the services (3–4). Sizes of community will influence how willing or able they may be to move to a new model or force some type of collective action. For example, CrossRef DOIs have been more successful than ORCID researcher IDs, because there are far more individual researchers than publishers. Even when the stakes are larger, tens of thousands of institutions are never going to get together on something the way ten countries will, even though the number of people affected is larger in the second scenario (Neylon 2017, 8).

Funders may anticipate long-term sustainability for projects through creating membership models where access to the tool created by the project is only available to members, but as scholarly communication increasingly favors open access, the access restriction must shift to more granular levels of access such as training sessions or conferences (Neylon 2017, 6). In open source library technology this approach has been used by ArchivesSpace, which restricts documentation access to members. Other projects rely on membership to allow access to the governance structure of the project.

That issue of governance and building financially effective structures is a challenge for any community project. Neylon suggests that templates for institutional models, such as the 2015 "Infrastructure Principles," help reduce the overhead for the collective action of building the institution. These principles include "transparency and community governance; financial sustainability, efficiency, and commitment to community needs; and mechanisms to protect integrity, as well as manage and mitigate the risk of failures" (7–8). Anticipating failure and worst-case scenarios should be part of planning, which is why case studies of projects that failed or struggled with success are so important to future efforts. We will look at some case studies like this in the next chapter.

Now we will turn to examining each type of community, each of which has specific benefits and challenges from both funding and community development perspectives. Using Neylon's analysis, we will see what types of sustainability can make sense for these projects, but in particular the challenges they are likely to face as they grow and change. In addition, for people who are looking to get involved in a community, there will be some ideas for getting started.

■ Small-scale Distributed Development

Small-scale distributed development projects tend to follow a traditional open source model, with the expectations that the users will be developers and that they will contribute back to the project, usually after running the system locally and spending time testing it. The types of community projects I found in my research included bibliographic management systems, content management systems, discovery layers, and library management systems of various kinds. Generally, such projects fill a certain niche because they grew out of a specific need. An individual or a small group needed to solve a problem, and began writing some code, which eventually found its way to an open source repository and required some level of governance about the decision-making.

Another type of group that may fall into the same patterns as a project focused on distributed development is a small discussion group where like-minded people try to create a new professional development group or develop new standards and practices. An example of something like this is the FORCE11 initiative for modernizing scholarly communications. Such groups may not do any development but will face a similar set of choices as they move forward.

Successful Projects and Benefits of This Model

Successful small-scale projects find uptake with libraries that have the development staff and time to work on projects and give back to the community. This makes sense according to the open source model that Raymond described. On the other hand, there are few if any examples of library-related projects whose original developer or institution was able to transfer ownership to another person or institution. Having the original developer involved in some way is helpful. One of the more successful small projects in library technology over the past ten years is VuFind, which is an open source OPAC that Villanova University released in 2007 and has used since 2008. The tool is in use worldwide, with over thirty active developers, but it maintains the character of a small project. Part of its success was early interest from large libraries that had tested VuFind (Nagy 2009), but because its institutional memory and support has been active over the past decade it does not have to rely solely on the community for new development.

Small projects can go the commercial route for sustainability but still retain a strong user governance community and an open source developer community. Omeka is a good example of this. Omeka is a digital collection platform first developed in 2007 by the Roy Rosenzweig Center for History and New Media (RRCHNM) with funding from the Institute of Museum and Library Services. Many libraries and museums rely on this tool to provide dynamic and standards-compliant digital exhibits. Although Omeka is still maintained by staff at the RRCHNM, an international community has driven development forward in new ways. In 2010, RRCHNM launched a hosted version of Omeka, called Omeka.net, which allowed institutions without local infrastructure to run Omeka. By offering this hosted service, RRCHNM can make it more likely that Omeka will be a self-sustaining platform (under the auspices of the Corporation for Digital Scholarship, a nonprofit corporation). The RRCHNM (2018) uses the same model for Zotero, a reference management tool, which relies on revenues from fee-based plans for document and citation hosting that go to funding development and operations.

Challenges of This Model

A small-scale project is in danger when it lacks governance and wider participation and will often stay in the hands of one or two developers that have a difficult time creating a truly distributed workflow and decision-making process. In traditional open source development, another interested developer that had shown interest and aptitude in the project could take over the work. But in my analysis of conference presentations in chapter 1, several of the projects that failed to make it fell into this pattern. Some had funding from commercial or federal sources and developed a tool that was in production at an institution or two but did not progress beyond that. Others developed tools that are still in use, but with no community to speak of. Without a community, any use of a tool means that any library choosing it must commit to taking on new development and contributing it back.

In many ways, this book grew out of experiences with small-scale projects that relied on the expertise of one or two people that failed to grow beyond initial potential or had slow and painful growth. Although growth is not always desirable, stagnation is not survivable. Changes in available technology in the larger world must be considered for library technology, and tools must be updated to meet new security requirements. One example is a solution that many libraries, including my own institution, adopted for displaying open hours. It was first published in the Code4Lib journal in 2008 and was informally supported by the Code4Lib community after that time. It relied on the Google Calendar API and used a connection among a Google Calendar, an SQL database, and PHP code to display the hours on the library website (Darby 2008). Although the setup took some time, the tool functioned well until November 2014, when Google deprecated the API that made this function, which required the code to be rewritten. For my institution in that moment, it made far more sense to go with a commercial product that had become available in the intervening years than to try to maintain that solution. The community was willing to help, but this illustrates the risk that such a solution entailed.

Even projects that are more community-based rather than technically based will have to adapt to change and agree how that change will happen. One example is a community called "Library Society of the World" (LSW), which emerged in 2007 as a tongue-in-cheek response to the American Library Association. Its main platform for discussion and community building was FriendFeed. In 2015, Facebook (which had acquired FriendFeed in 2009) shut down the platform, which was a shock to those who relied on that community. Eventually LSW members settled on a new platform, called Mokum, in 2016. For at least some of the original members, the community maintained the personal connection and humor that had always been important independent of the platform (Jastram 2018).

Opportunities for Engagement

Small-scale distributed development projects may be the first thing that people picture when they think of community technology projects, and yet participating in such projects may be the most challenging for someone new to technology circles or to library work. Knowing why you would need a specialized tool requires some experience in libraries, and for those without much technology experience, writing and testing code aspects of participation will be a barrier to entry. For this reason, communities should ensure that there is an easy path to understanding what a certain tool is intended to do, and the technology required to work with it. Documentation should include all the languages used in the tool, tutorials for learning the basics, and a clear and kind path for how someone new to the work can get started.

People who are looking to advance their technical skills to move into a different career area will find it most valuable to spend time on small-scale distributed development. For example, perhaps someone with limited technical skills can start by writing documentation or doing simple bug fixes as they build the skills and reputation that can lead to larger opportunities. In general, interested and committed contributors who want to learn should be able to start small to learn to improve tools that they use in their jobs.

Specific task support should include, at minimum, technical documentation and a developer mailing list. Another useful practice is having routine orientation calls or webinars to help new participants get acquainted with the programming languages, tools (such as version control), and the technical decision-making process. For new members of the community, this is essential, but even for seasoned contributors these calls can be helpful reminders of practices that may be easy to forget in the excitement of work.

■ User Groups

User groups are usually based around a specific product or project, and sometimes might be a type of product working group or community advisory board. Such groups deserve special focus because they are often the most accessible to the widest variety of participants. Even the smallest libraries need some type of technology, and for those without many technical resources in-house, participating in a user group allows them to draw on the collective wisdom of all users. Community can form around anything, no matter how "official" the organization or how corporate the product is.

From something as formal as an officially incorporated user group, to an informal e-mail discussion list, or even a social media hashtag, such communities can provide vital support for tools or library processes. In some cases, participating in such groups allows all users to have a measure of governance over the product, whether commercial or open source.

Table 4.1 describes the user groups that represent the vendors with the largest share of the ILS market in 2018.

TABLE 4.1

NORTH AMERICAN USER GROUPS FOR ILS VENDORS

Vendor	User Group Name (North American)	Type
Ex Libris	ELUNA (Ex Libris Users of North America)	Independent nonprofit; support and enhancement requests
Innovative Interfaces	Innovative Users Group	Independent nonprofit; support and enhancement requests
OCLC	WMS Global Community and User Group Meetings	Maintained by OCLC; support
SirsiDynix	COSUGI (Customers of SirsiDynix User Group, Inc., North America)	Independent nonprofit; support and enhancement requests

Successful Projects and Benefits

As table 4.1 illustrates, many user groups have a specific role in governing enhancement requests for vendors. I can speak from my own experience working at a library that is an Ex Libris customer. The Ex Libris Users of North America (ELUNA) and International Group of Ex Libris Users (IGeLU) represent the Ex Libris customer community. These groups have a formal relationship with Ex Libris and an agreement in place about how the groups will interact with each other and Ex Libris (ELUNA 2018). One concrete result of this is an enhancement request system that relies on community votes. Ex Libris developers rank the enhancement requests by difficulty, and after another vote the final selections are put on the development plan. This process ensures that at least some community-valued features make it into the product. Another mechanism outside the groups that Ex Libris provides for customers is "Idea Exchange," which allows anyone to post an idea and others in the community to vote for it. These ideas are not guaranteed to be implemented even if they receive a significant number of votes, but Idea Exchange does help illustrate what needs are, and sometimes these ideas are implemented.

Even when there is no explicit governance mechanism, user groups allow the sharing of ideas and can also allow a vendor to receive feedback or share information in a more informal manner. User group meetings can be independent gatherings organized by customers that take place regionally or at larger conferences. And in some cases, the group may exist online or through a mailing list. In general, participating in such groups is a good investment of resources, whether that investment is in the form of money to travel to meetings or simply time to participate in online discussions.

Participating in this type of give-and-take is beneficial for both companies and customers. For customers who have either limited options in the market and/or platform lock-in, giving constructive feedback and criticism to a vendor is the only way to ensure a more satisfactory product. For companies, this process represents active and continual focus groups and set of beta testers. Companies that take a page from open source development value their active users and ensure they have a space to share their feedback.

Customers working together can also convince companies to take new approaches. In late 2013, a group discussion on the bepress Digital Commons mailing list resulted in a set of customer demands that forced the company to acknowledge that it had not been transparent enough about its development road map. The CEO of bepress responded with a promise to provide more information and confirm that the list of feature requests was mostly in process (Bankier 2013a). More frequent development-road-map blog posts followed (Bankier 2013b). After Elsevier acquired bepress, which was announced publicly before being announced to customers, that dynamic of intense customer questioning and the corresponding response from the company continued on the mailing list (Bankier 2017). bepress established the bepress Advisory Board in 2018. Made up of members representing customers from several library types, this board is designed to formalize the relationship between bepress and the user group by creating guiding principles, shaping product innovation, and ensuring that even with access to additional resources from Elsevier, the core focus of the product is maintained (Bruns, Badertscher, and Yeh 2018). Such an evolution from mailing list to formal demands to governance structure is not unique to this community and serves as a good example of how companies ensuring a strong user focus could avoid making the same mistakes.

Another perhaps unexpected benefit for commercial enterprises to develop such user groups is that it allows them to find customers with the most experience and interest in the product, and then hire them as developers or for support roles. Because so many early ILSs were developed as close partnerships between librarians and programmers, it has always been likely that the active users would be attracted to jobs with the company, and that the company would want to hire them. This is particularly the case because these early jobs were avenues to some travel and adventure in addition to the challenges of systems librarianship (Syed 2011, 36).

Even as systems librarianship and related areas have become more stable, this mixing between customers and their vendors continues. As we know from chapter 3's discussion of motivations for participating in open source communities, developers have always had an expectation that working for free could lead to job opportunities. The same is true in library technology. Springshare has hired several librarians who were active in online discussions about its products. Laura Harris mentions that one of the main reasons she joined the company when it offered her a job is that she had already developed such a strong relationship with it (L. Harris 2016).

Challenges of This Model

On the consumer side, creating such groups outside of official channels or adapting the official channels allows the community to ask for change from the organization around which they have formed. Although this is not the case across library technology, the trend toward conglomeration means that the number of vendors for integrated library systems has shrunk markedly over the years. In 1990, Library Technology Reports had reports on twenty-four microcomputer (in contrast to the earlier minicomputer) automated library systems, which were installed in some 27,000 libraries (up from 1,000 installations in 1986) (Matthews, Williams, and Wilson 1990). Although some of those vendors in business in 1990 still exist, generally they do not function in the same way or with the same name. Marshall Breeding's recent graphical report on mergers and acquisitions shows a clear trend for mergers, with effectively four vendors controlling most of the ILS market: ProQuest, Innovative Interfaces, SirsiDynix, and OCLC.

With limited market pressure on the ILS market, it is up to the community to work together to ensure that products move forward in an appropriate manner. Products should be open enough that a developer community can form around them, and libraries can develop creative solutions to problems without waiting for a vendor.

Opportunities for Engagement

The type of user group affects the level of commitment a library or an individual should expect to find in a community. A user group with a membership fee and governance responsibilities will require more effort, but also provide more support than an informal mailing list. Yet for most libraries, the reality is that commercial products form the bulk of its technology budget and staff resources, and therefore, spending time in user group communities, however informal, is a worthwhile investment. Getting started with such groups can be as easy as joining a mailing list and making it a habit to ask and answer questions, write up solutions on a blog, and stay up-to-date with new releases. For formal membership-based user groups, there are opportunities and expectations for participating in governance.

User groups can additionally help to provide emotional support beyond the task support that is officially provided by documentation, discussion lists, and trainings. In one sense, it seems wrong that groups should need to self-organize around a large corporate entity that should be putting their own resources into developing communities, but in practice, those large corporate entities underwrite a good deal of digital library community. In some cases, there are specific community manager roles to facilitate this type of community building, for instance, at OCLC. Whether it is funding conferences or having staff time allocated to development of open source projects (such as EBSCO and FOLIO), those companies often see value in building communities that ultimately drive or facilitate the use of their products.

■ General Technology Associations and Consortiums

As we saw in chapter 1, associations and consortiums form to formalize technical partnerships or discussions. Some of these are to solve specific problems, but the problems keep changing. For that reason, new partnerships are always springing up as needs change. Managing these associations takes special effort to balance long-term adherence to mission with meeting member needs over time. The specific practices that these types of organizations undertake vary, and we will look at the tools they may use in later chapters. In general, however, these groups have the potential to have a larger impact because their scope is larger. They can focus on many types of projects and have a wide membership that can learn from each other.

Successful Projects and Benefits of This Model

Some of the better-known examples of these general technology associations and consortiums are the divisions of the American Library Association that have technology-related programming (which by now is nearly all of them). The Society of American Archivists has multiple sections related to web archiving, electronic records, digital preservation, and many other technologies. The Digital Library Federation, which is a division of the Council on Library and Information Resources (CLIR), is another important association in library technology, particularly around digital collections and digital preservation, though it supports all areas of library technology. DLF was founded as a collaborative project in 1995 by multiple research libraries to support the growing need for research into digital library platforms and services. As these two examples indicate, associations and consortiums have generally needed to remain flexible over the years as newer communities such as Code4Lib have emerged. Moreover, they must also maintain their adaptiveness by finding avenues for partnerships and mutual support.

Regional consortial networks have needed to evolve over the years. The impetus for networks such as these was originally for cooperative cataloging, in some cases dating back to the Great Depression (LYRASIS 2016). In the 1970s existing networks retooled and new ones formed to replicate OCLC's services in other regions beyond Ohio, though at least for SOLINET, the southeastern network founded in 1973, this quickly turned to contracting for services from OCLC rather than re-creating the system (Gribbin 1988). Other networks, such as Illinois Library Computer Systems Organization (ILSCO) (founded in 1980), formed to create a statewide ILS (CARLI 2018). By the mid-2000s, however, the needs of regional networks had changed. SOLINET merged in 2009 with PALINET (comprised mostly of mid-Atlantic states) to create LYRASIS, based on the recognition that a larger scale would help members (and the merger was speeded along because of the 2008 economic crisis) (Freeman 2009). ILSCO merged with other state cooperatives that handled collection services, grants, and electronic resources licensing to form CARLI in 2005. Another scenario was the Research Libraries Group (RLG), which formed in 1974 by research libraries in place of OCLC's services and based at Stanford (using the system that Stanford had developed). RLG merged with OCLC in 2006 and integrated many of its research programs into OCLC Research (OCLC 2015). OCLC has similarly absorbed other entities throughout the years, either as strategic mergers or as part of bankruptcy proceedings (OCLC 2017).

The challenges that faced libraries in the 1970s to automate and integrate their technology with other libraries still face libraries that need to build, expand, and preserve digital collections that are integrated with other collections and the web. Networks had to update their services or merge with other networks that could provide those services. The complexity of hosting and maintaining many digital library platforms, particularly for small libraries, means that regional consortiums will likely always play an important role in library technology while they support these platforms. We will address some specific issues in the next section, but for now, we can note that although organizations may have originally supported one specific open source project, they can still expand their services to meet new needs. An example of this is DuraSpace, which formed in 2009 from two separate open source project governance organizations. Fedora Commons, formed in 2007, governed the Fedora Project digital repository software. The DSpace Foundation also formed in 2007 out of an earlier DSpace governance organization. Because both organizations had similar membership and aims, they merged in 2009 and remain the governance organization for DSpace, Fedora, and VIVO. As part of its move to sustainability, it established the DuraCloud subscription service, which is a way to combine open source tools in a hosted solution. By 2014, DuraSpace managed to be self-sustaining with no grant funding and required lower cost membership fees for institutions from developing nations (LYRASIS 2018, 30). In 2016, DuraSpace and LYRASIS announced a planned merger, but this fell apart after a few months of official talks because of missions that were hard to reconcile (Enis 2016).

Finally, the wider technology community provides many examples of governance, which in some cases directly govern tools that libraries use heavily. The Apache Software Foundation was formed in 1999 and is the governance organization for 350 open source projects. When the original developers of the HTTPD web server were no longer working on the project, a group got together and built this out into what is still the leading web server software. The methods that the ASF and the Apache projects use for decision-making are based on a well-defined meritocracy with multiple layers that include users, developers, and committers. Developers and committers can be elected as members of a Project Management Committee that makes major decisions about the evolution of the project and has oversight of legal matters (Apache Software Foundation 2018).

Challenges of This Model

Because they are such large operations, associations can lack flexibility to shift focus and entail some inherent risks. For example, the New Media Consortium (NMC) was an association started in 1993 to promote technology in education. It created the highly regarded Horizon Reports and a series of educational technology conferences, but abruptly shut down in 2017 due to financial mismanagement. EDUCAUSE purchased the assets of the NMC and is working on maintaining the Horizon Reports and conferences, but the future of both remain uncertain (McKenzie 2018).

Associations must prove to potential members that the benefits for joining, and the collective action that joining will create, are compelling enough to justify spending limited professional development or organizational membership funds. Because of the duplication of effort and costs of reaching out to the same limited pool of members, associations may have to merge to remain viable. In 2018, several divisions of the American Library Association—LITA, ALCTS, and LLAMA—issued a white paper that explored merging divisions (Yelton 2018). Such a merger, if it eventually occurs, will be an important test of the shift from a more focused to a more general association, as has been the trend throughout the history of library associations, particularly in technology. The challenge for new associations will be to retain members with a specialized professional focus while offering more value to all members. But just as Ralph Parker predicted for the fate of the small library, the small general technology group may also not exist in the future.

Opportunities for Engagement

Getting involved with general associations and consortiums ranges in difficulty, but usually there are many types of opportunities to become involved with the work of an organization. A good starting place is a working group or interest group, which may not require any formal membership to participate, though access to in-person meetings or mailing lists may be restricted to members. For those trying to get an idea of the culture of an organization, this can be a low-stakes path. For those who want (or need for the purposes of promotion or tenure) greater involvement, many more committed opportunities are available. All associations have committees or task forces, which may be actively seeking volunteers. These are good starting places for people who have an interest in learning more about governance or a technology but would not be able to jump into development work on a specific product. And finally, although the boards or other leadership groups of associations require a good deal of commitment, they are for many an appropriate next step because they provide leadership opportunities that may not be available in their day jobs. As all the mergers and shifts in focus illustrate, associations must constantly evolve as technology and society change. Participating in this type of governance provides a number of enlightening challenges.

Associations are in some ways the easiest type of community to understand. They have a stated mission, set of programs, and clear ways to get involved. Paying a membership fee should give some benefits, and many of these benefits become one of the "collective goods" previously discussed, such as new technology standards or white papers. On the other hand, a large association with many smaller communities can be inscrutable to outsiders, who may need to spend several years learning the structure and experimenting with different working groups, interest groups, committees, or task forces to find an appropriate niche. Associations will benefit themselves and their memberships by streamlining this process. Supports that would be helpful include providing detailed documentation about membership benefits, types of opportunities available to members (and nonmembers), and a clear statement of the collective goods produced by that association and made possible by members.

Associations should provide as many task-support mechanisms as possible, particularly items like mailing lists, videoconferencing platforms, and document repositories that provide tangible benefits to members and help them to create their own smaller communities within the larger community. Because many members join such associations specifically for the emotional-support component, associations should meet this need through measures such as being active on social media, planning virtual and in-person gatherings, and developing a strong user-focused culture.

■ Large Projects

The concept of a "large" project is, in some ways, not all that different from a general association, but I reference it here in contrast to the small-scale distributed development project. Large projects occur when a small-scale project is successful enough that many others want to join in, or its very nature requires some amount of governance to function because it requires sharing of resources among institutions, whether infrastructure, personnel, or materials. The latter sometimes grows out of a grant-funded project to create shared infrastructure, or sometimes after some small-scale experiments prove the need for larger infrastructure. It can be difficult to tell when what was once a small-scale distributed project is now a large project, but communities feeling growing pains may need to add an additional level of governance to ensure projects succeed.

Successful Projects and Benefits of This Model

We will look at several large projects in the case studies to follow, but the overarching achievement of successful projects is that they benefit their members enough to secure funding past the initial start-up phase. The benefits mean that participating institutions or individuals receive infrastructure or a new tool they could never have developed on their own, or for a lower cost than a commercial service.

Mirroring the adoption and support for open source development in the larger technology world, some library projects achieve sustainability through purchase or support by a larger commercial enterprise. Such was the case for the library services platform FOLIO, which was based on the Kuali OLE initiative. Like many other projects (several of which we will examine in the case studies), FOLIO originated in a 2008 planning process funded by the Mellon Foundation. Under the umbrella of the Kuali

Foundation, Mellon and nine partner institutions provided funding for ongoing development (OLE 2018). The Kuali OLE software was developed by this partnership and installed at three partner institutions. It had slow uptake beyond the partner institutions because of its complexity and the increasing expectation of multitenant Software as a Service (SaaS) that it lacked. EBSCO saw this as an opportunity to support open source development for a library services platform that could work with their EDS discovery layer and drive competition in the marketplace. Along with IndexData, EBSCO stepped in to provide monetary support to the community and expertise to develop an entirely new product in the tradition of Kuali OLE, while leaving the governance of the project within the community (Breeding 2016). In the commercial world it is normal for a group to do conceptual work that is acquired by another company—for example, Facebook and Apple frequently acquire small start-ups for their intellectual property, and certainly traditional library vendors are not strangers to this practice. For the library world such a partnership is an encouraging model for continued development of open source SaaS products in libraries.

Another twist on a sustainability model is hosted consortial versions of open source software. Even with mergers of networks over the past decades, it is possible to retain some characteristics of a small project while drawing on the governance and scale of the consortium. The Evergreen ILS open source community provides an example. The Georgia Public Library System started developing its own ILS in 2006, which eventually became the PINES consortial catalog. The software as a whole is a vibrant open source project, which developed a strong user and developer community over the years (Evergreen Project 2013).

Challenges to This Model

Large development projects have the possibility of existing in their own spheres. Institutions that need a specific set of services developed band together to make this happen, and should they be successful, the tools are likely to be of most use to those members. Expanding the community can be a challenge if all potential participants are already involved, and adoption outside of that group is too expensive or challenging for potential additional members. Unless the project can figure out a way to make additional institutions able to use the product, such as developing a consortial hosting or

SaaS model, the community's membership will necessarily remain static. This is not necessarily a bad thing but will limit the participant base.

Several large distributed projects that have existed independently (with or without grant funding) for several years, but with reliance on large research universities to fund them and participate in the communities and development. Different types of institutions may therefore face limitations on what open source software is available to them. A major example of this is Samvera (formerly Hydra), which will receive more in-depth examination in the next chapter. One of the Samvera components, Avalon Media System, is a project codeveloped and maintained by Northwestern University and Indiana University, and implemented by several institutions. Yet its complexity means that its uptake will necessarily be slow by institutions without a full development staff, a reality illustrated well at a Code4Lib conference in 2014 with a map of the technical dependencies (Klein and Rudder 2014). The message of that presentation, and of others like it, is that anyone building tools and governance structures for library technology must make it possible for all types of librarians and libraries to participate by making installation and maintenance as simple as possible or developing low-cost and straightforward SaaS options.

Opportunities for Engagement

Potential ways of engaging with large projects will certainly depend on the type of project. In most cases, however, there are opportunities to participate on either the development side or the governance side. This can be a tricky balance, however, because for projects that are mostly restricted to members, participating as a user-developer will depend on the institutional commitment. Would-be developers are put in awkward positions if their expertise is for developing in one programming language and their institution switches to a new technical solution. In general, however, large projects offer opportunities similar to small projects in terms of writing documentation or participating in open source development, and similar to associations in terms of serving on committees or boards.

Membership models that allow all members to participate in governance while supporting specific funds for developers can be successful. One example is the ArchivesSpace community, which requires membership prior to participation in the community, including the ability to access documentation (ArchivesSpace 2018). The software is free to use but necessitates a good deal of extra work to implement without access to the official community. There are downsides to such a model, but clarity about the amount of money it takes to support software is useful when the alternative is too restrictive. Like associations, a clear definition of the benefits available to members and the collective goods created by that membership will help in making the decision to join or not.

The amount of infrastructure required means that creating these models or expectations for partnerships needs to be an ongoing and participatory process. One model is the Code4Lib Fiscal Continuity Interest Group, which held a multiyear conversation with the community and researched various options. Those options culminated in a community vote to decide upon on the preferred option, which was to partner with DLF as a fiscal agent for the community and its conference.

Because large projects tend to be technically onerous, it is important to offer ample documentation at all levels. Like small-scale distributed development, there should be orientations to the technologies used, the decision-making processes, and the community norms. Large communities must have codes of conduct, whether or not they have in-person gatherings, and should not only recognize that their users and members will be organizing meetups at other events, but also determine which code of conduct applies should that occur. Emotional support may be particularly necessary for members of these communities, who may find themselves in awkward situations, either as technical people trying to explain the need for the project to institutional administrators, or as nontechnical people participating in governance of the project.

■ Finding a Place in the Community Landscape

Few community technology projects have an identified trajectory when they begin. Most projects start as small conversations and pilots, which may be highly experimental. Some projects may combine several approaches. For example, a large digital preservation network with a governing board will encompass smaller open source software components and user groups. General associations or consortia could adopt the practices of small-scale distributed development that encourage the users (or members) to be developers (or leaders).

For people looking to get involved in a community project, the landscape provides multiple entry points, which can be overwhelming. Returning to the idea of motivation, different types of opportunities will mesh with different motivations. And, just as projects may be experimental, an individual may have to experiment and try several things before finding the right fit. Projects with good community management practices should be able to slot people into likely opportunities and make it clear to those coming in from the outside what is available. Going into a project understanding where it fits in the community landscape and what successful projects have done will help with this process.

CHAPTER 5

CASE STUDIES

U sing best practices with real projects is not as simple as following a formula. Projects that have done everything "right" may not succeed, and projects that look like they should fail nevertheless manage to succeed. The following case studies are intended to put best practices in perspective across the community landscape.

These four projects are worth considering together because they share similar origin stories. Except for DPLA, they all originated in 2008, and all began at the juncture of mass digitization and cloud computing becoming far more mainstream. In the 1970s, online distributed computing became available for the first time. The mid-2000s saw the advent of cloud computing as we now understand it, with the launch of Amazon Elastic Cloud in 2006 (Miller 2016). The following projects come out of that same spirit of distributed computing, and although the idea of "cloud computing" was somewhat abstract in 2008, by now it has become the norm.

Three of the projects are still successful and functioning; one was disbanded after only a few years. However, all of them experienced missteps, growing pains, and challenges. Understanding what failed, and why, is critical to form better communities in the future. Without honest and open discussions among participants it becomes easy to forget the past and assume that next time will be different. (The same goes for any project, not just community projects.) It is true that even when it seems politically expedient to pretend everything is going fine, projects will not succeed if there are problems (whether technical or political) that are not fixed.

In these case studies I will briefly describe what the project was or is intended to do; the origin and current status of the project, which includes the challenges that it will face moving forward after its first decade; and lessons that other communities can learn from these projects.

■ Project Bamboo

Writing a description of what exactly Project Bamboo was remains a challenge, as highlighted by its biographer, Quinn Dombrowski, who was closely tied to the project and thus in an excellent position to write an honest post-mortem, simply titled "Whatever Happened to Project Bamboo?" The shortest description is that the project was an attempt to solve digital humanities research infrastructure problems at scale, that is, those that would serve the needs of institutions supporting digital humanities research projects.

Origins, Challenges, and Current Status

Despite what looked like the best conditions at the outset, including funding from the Mellon Foundation that allowed for paid staff and partners from major research universities, Project Bamboo only lasted from 2008 until 2012. Anyone planning a large technology project should learn from its example.

The origin of Project Bamboo grew from the realization of academic technologists that many digital humanities infrastructure needs were not, or did not need to be, unique to individual institutions or scholars. Rather than spending time and money setting up a research infrastructure for individual scholars, it seemed worthwhile to invest in a set of common services that could be used across institutions. Funders might find such services attractive because they would not have to fund the same basic infrastructure costs for each new project (Dombrowski 2014b, 327).

The academic technology experts who started the project had a vision of a web service–oriented architecture that would allow various components to work together and gathered a large group for Mellon-funded planning workshops. The group was purposely divided among all the constituents of a digital humanities project, including scholars, librarians, and academic technologists, and was designed to bring individuals together to solve problems in new ways. The thought was that scholars would share their problems, and the technologists and librarians would try to solve them technically. This presupposed that their problems could be solved with technical solutions (328). This did not seem to be the case after the first planning workshop, and as Dombrowski points out, the flexibility and participatory design vision for the project were only so far as they matched the service-oriented architecture that was the initial vision for the project (Dombrowski 2014b, 333).

Nevertheless, a good deal of technical work was accomplished during an eighteen-month development period, which left the community with some hope that the project would gain additional funding. Ultimately the lack of resources, definition, uptake, and retention meant that Mellon declined to fund any more work, and asked Project Bamboo to archive the project components for use by others (Dombrowski 2014b, 332).

The major piece of the project that is still in use is the DiRT Directory, which was an already extant tool that Project Bamboo adopted. It is a directory of tools and services for digital humanists, organized by the type of work performed and stage of project. The DiRT Directory is overseen by both scholars and librarians with digital humanities expertise (Dombrowski 2014a). Given this, it seems likely that improving this directory was what everyone actually needed, and with the advent of cloud computing, containerization (i.e., the ability to create virtual machines with different operating systems and configurations that can be distributed), and the more widespread use of APIs (which help connect data between systems), it became easier for individuals to find ways to connect tools with minimal technical support. Although there is still a great need for academic technology support for digital humanities, the infrastructure piece is no longer the challenge that it was.

Types of Support Offered

Although Project Bamboo got it "right" about which types of support were offered, it yields some useful illustrations of how having the right platforms for support is not enough to support the needs of volunteers and their engagement. Task-oriented support consisted of a wiki with extensive documentation, an issue tracker, and a code repository. Emotional-oriented support included a blog. Dombrowski pointed out in her article that in all these cases there were warning signs when these tools were used (2014b). For example, the blog was not updated for eighteen months during the intense work phase, which led people to doubt the project was still going. Communication to participants was hampered by a lack of shared vision and a strong mission. The wiki did not receive much use during the planning phase, which was originally blamed on the complexity of wiki syntax, but Dombrowski suggests it was in fact because participants did not see a compelling reason to use it. Their problems were too abstract to be boiled down to defining a service-oriented architecture, an idea that was off-putting to many participants.

Lessons to Learn

Future community projects can take several useful lessons from the demise of Project Bamboo. Although it was intended to be a community design process, too much was preordained by the project plan. The scholars who were the intended audience of this work did not find it a useful or compelling vision, and there was no way to get the technical and scholarly pieces working together in a useful way before the money and energy ran out. Although this was an attempt at shared governance and participatory design, it lacked the shared vision or language needed to have the conversation. "The project struggled to identify a coherent vision that neatly encapsulated all the work being done in the name of Bamboo, or to clearly describe what future state the work would collectively realize" (Dombrowski 2014b, 331).

Something like Project Bamboo can suffer from the types of problems that beset associations when they must remain sufficiently general to meet a wide variety of needs but have a number of specific initiatives to meet their mission or the needs of members—flexibility is only practical up to a point, after which it becomes generic and uncompelling. The project looked like it had many external and internal factors that should have led to success, such as funding from Mellon, a staff, a wiki, documentation, and a blog. But because it was not solving the actual problems that the participants had, they lacked the emotional engagement to maintain motivation other than for the most compelling pieces of the project (such as the DiRT Directory). With a heavy reliance on institutional memory and siloed work groups, participants lacked task support as the project went on. Funders of large digital projects may ask for sustainability plans for technical infrastructure, but there is more to the long-term success of community projects than that.

■ HathiTrust

HathiTrust is a collective attempt to digitize research libraries at scale. Begun in 2008, it was a partnership among large research universities (primarily in what was then known as the Committee for Institutional Cooperation [CIC], now known as the Big Ten Academic Alliance) to develop a shared infrastructure for preserving digitized books and their metadata. Its approach was also similar in some ways, but ultimately it was able to turn some of the same liabilities as Project Bamboo into successes.

Origins, Challenges, and Current Status

According to a FAQ page created by the University of Michigan in August 2005, the project began as an official partnership in 2004 between Google and the University of Michigan to scan all the books in Michigan's collection. The project, known originally as MDP, was estimated to take six years to scan seven million books. This was Google's first effort creating Google Books (at the time known as Google Print). The reasons for the partnership were stated as both altruistic—making knowledge more open to the public, and pragmatic—the university's scanning program could only achieve 5,000 books a year to Google's tens of thousands per week. Google's exact methods were kept secret, but they were designed to do no harm to the materials and allow them to be reshelved immediately. The FAQ goes on to answer the question of "Legal Issues," with a statement that the project did, so far as it understood, comply with copyright law and that scanning was in itself not a violation. It emphasized this by stating that the aim of the project was, in addition to sharing knowledge, preserving the materials.

Michigan planned to keep its own copies separate from Google in order to curate and preserve the collection, as well as to provide digital access to authorized users (University of Michigan Library 2005). The desire to maintain local copies of the scans was the impetus to create partnerships. There was no cost-effective way to maintain multiple copies in multiple locations for proper preservation, and partnerships to create a better digital infrastructure—a shared digital repository—would be the way to address this. From the outset, Michigan thought of creating partnerships with other CIC institutions, though the discussions moved slowly.

A culture clash between technologists and librarians threatened the project, just as had happened with Project Bamboo. The librarians came at the project with "a culture of collectivism and egalitarianism that was integral to the identity of librarians and which libraries had thrived upon for centuries" (Centivany 2017, 2361). Yet this approach seemed to postpone ever making a final decision and caused negotiations to stall.

At this juncture, a personal relationship between administrators at the University of Michigan and Indiana University helped get talks restarted. With a few phone calls and some plain language, they hammered out an agreement between the two institutions to share the development and cost for building the repository, with Michigan handling all the decision-making for the partnership. This was, as Centivany quotes the Indiana administrator saying, "a bit of a countercultural moment in higher education" (2363). Yet this worked because the two institutions had a "charmed" relationship with a set of shared values, temperaments, and a history of collaboration. Building on this relationship to go outside of the CIC was a potential disaster, however, as the rest of the CIC saw it as a betrayal of community norms of consensus and collectivism (2363).

Now that the technical issues were on the way to being solved, the future of HathiTrust required dealing with the political ramifications of the partnership. Michigan and Indiana had originally told CIC members they would be "secondary partners," but decided that the public announcement and face of HathiTrust would be as an equal partnership of all founding institutions, with shared governance roles on the board. They also looked for partners outside the CIC to expand the impact of the project (Centivany 2017, 2364). After some lengthy discussions, the University of California system and the California Digital Library (CDL) joined HathiTrust, partly due to economic considerations, but also for the political power that being a founding member would afford. While wielding this as a political tool to form the project, it was necessary to change the project's approach for the future of the partnership. Centivany reports a participant stating that for people to trust Michigan "we had to give HathiTrust over to the members of the community, so they could settle upon what HathiTrust might become" (2365). That decision to step back from power put the idea of the community in the forefront of participants' minds and made a new collective possible.

As of 2018, ten years after forming, HathiTrust has six consortia and state systems, and 140 individual members, ranging from large state universities to small liberal arts colleges and including some international partners. A Board of Governors (with six members appointed from founding institutions, six elected from all institutions) and CEO oversee HathiTrust, an arrangement that has been in place since 2012. The project is actively seeking new partnerships with "academic and research libraries with large amounts of digitized...content or substantial print collections" (HathiTrust Digital Library). Given that the benefits for participating are largely around digital preservation and access of institutional content, this definition of who is a beneficial partner makes sense.

Of course, without being a member, access to the community—and therefore the data—is limited to public domain works. The exception is the HathiTrust Research Center, which allows access for researchers to the HathiTrust corpus for nonconsumptive scholarship that falls within parameters for fair use for textual analysis (HathiTrust Research Center). *Authors Guild v. HathiTrust* indicated in 2014 that the scanning project was a transformative use of the content, and therefore fell under fair use (which was the same ruling for the *Authors Guild v. Google* case in 2015) (McSherry 2015). Yet this means that access to all the data must be restricted, and based on legitimate fair use cases, such as access for the print-disabled.

Types of Support Offered

HathiTrust has a help guide aimed at general users, active if slow-paced social media accounts, and a blog that has existed since the beginning of the project. With a tagline of "There's an elephant in the library," the somewhat subversive nature of the whole enterprise remains at the forefront. For potential members, there are several pages of descriptions of what membership entails, and some details about technical specifications and processes. A "HathiTrust Digital Library Profile" gives details on the viability of the project from technical, institutional, and financial perspectives.

Lessons to Learn

There was no reason to suspect that HathiTrust would fare better than Project Bamboo, given that Project Bamboo also had strong funding and a participatory outlook from the beginning. Two factors indicate why this might have been. The reality of storing and preserving digital content and providing access to a corpus of data was a solvable problem with a relatively clear way forward, and therefore easier to define than Project Bamboo. The strong personal relationship between the administrators at Michigan and Indiana that ended up making HathiTrust possible could have ended it just as easily if it had not been transferred to a collective vision to solve a problem. What Centivany's and Dombrowski's work proves is that all communities have a "dark" history. Behind every community project are conversations, meetings, and management decisions that the rest of us cannot see or understand. Thus the "failures" may not be about any decision the community made about how to run itself, but on outside forces over which no one had control. Communities can adapt to those outside forces in some cases, but this requires a good deal of community buy-in and political will.

Full partnership in HathiTrust will probably remain out of reach for most institutions that do not have the type of collections that are served well by that scale. The existence of the collections, even without full access to in-copyright materials, does enrich the entire library and scholarly community. This project has made access to older materials much better, and the corpus in the HTRC allows computational access that would be impossible otherwise. Although altruistic motivations for participating in community projects vary, highlighting obvious benefits of this type should make a case for participating in any similar community project.

■ Samvera Community (Previously Project Hydra)

Samvera is a set of tools used with the Fedora digital asset management platform, originally created in the late 1990s at Cornell University. It allows institutions to create repositories for preserving materials and managing metadata, and more importantly, to share workflows across institutions. Creating new features that will work for multiple institutions is a complex undertaking and must be approached that way from the outset for success. From the beginning, the point was to work collaboratively and intentionally build a community ("Community Framework").

Origins, Challenges, and Current Status

In 2008, four partners—the University of Hull, University of Virginia, Stanford University, and Fedora Commons (now known as DuraSpace)—came together to build open source repository components on top of the Fedora repository software. At the time, this project became known as Project Hydra, which is an allusion to the multiple heads of Hydra, the mythical creature. This reflected both the way the tools worked and the community nature of the project. Fedora had existed since 1997 but had not become more widely useful until 2003 after a Mellon Foundation-funded project between the University of Virginia and Cornell University got it to a point where multiple institutions could use it. Unlike DSpace (developed at the Massachusetts Institute of Technology) and EPrints (developed at the University of Southampton), which were primarily designed to be open access scholarly repositories and had features to support that aim, Fedora was always designed to be a flexible framework that was about features important to manage digital content in general (the original acronym was Flexible Extensible Digital Object Repository Architecture). What happened with that content was up to the developers at each institution, and with that flexibility came complexity. For Hull, choosing Fedora was a better solution than the other repository frameworks as it would allow it to change its approaches as new requests for services and new types of content came along.

But because many institutions needed to end up in the same place anyway, it would be more practical to work together to build common solutions. Chris Awre and Richard Green (2017), writing to commemorate nearly ten years of the project, described its origins as a discussion among interested institutions at a conference in 2008 that led to ongoing meetings among the four original institutions and an additional partner. The idea at the time was not to create a new open source community, but just to work together on making useful tools for Fedora. Over the next eighteen months these meetings continued until by spring of 2010 the approach was set, and by late 2011 working versions of Hydra were available. At this point, the popularity of the software grew, and many institutions wanted to become partners. The original partners formed a steering committee and developed a formal commitment process to establish new partners.

Throughout the early period of Samvera, the goal was to avoid becoming "another open source flash in the pan" (Awre and Green 2017, 84) by taking a deliberate approach to software, and later to community development.

For example, the Hydra Connect conference, started in 2014, came out of a realization that institutions might want to use Hydra and share their solutions without being able to commit to a partnership. In 2017, there were thirty-five Hydra Partners, around seventy known users, and ninety institutions represented at the conference, so this trend has continued. The developer community has included at least fifty different individuals and works on the Apache model of individual and, for the employing institutions, corporate contributor licenses (Awre and Green 2017, 84). The name "Samvera" was forced by a trademark dispute. The Icelandic word for "togetherness," Samvera exemplifies what was best about the community, rather than the software, as well as metaphorically bridging the American and European members of the community (Awre and Green 2017, 86).

The complexity of a flexible framework remains. For institutions that need a repository solution out of the box, the overhead can still be too much. Solving that problem was the origin story for the product now known as Hyku, which is the product that came out of the Hydra-in-a-Box project. The need was due to smaller institutions requiring a tool to create a digital repository for their collections to ingest them into DPLA (about which more later). The project was funded by IMLS and was a collaboration among DPLA, Stanford, and DuraSpace. Funding on the project ran between 2015 and 2017, but work on additional aspects that are important to DPLA functionality, such as harvest and ingest tools, continues (Della Bitta and Shepherd 2017). The Hydra-in-a-Box project was successful in generating community input, with around 200 people helping on the project in some way (Hydra-in-a-Box Team 2017). Hyku is based on Hyrax, which is an amalgamation of other Samvera repository approaches (most notably Sufia, which was a direct-deposit repository tool built by Pennsylvania State University), and how one would go about adopting this tool remains somewhat unclear, though DuraSpace does plan to offer a hosted version called "HykuDirect."

What the list of tools and changes in approaches illustrates well is that despite best intentions, Samvera lacks a clear path to using the software at institutions that lack robust technical staff. Not all partner institutions or users of the software are at well-funded research institutions, but nevertheless implementing and maintaining the Fedora Commons repository and the Samvera framework are not a simple task. Changes in the technical approaches to the major modules and the need to keep up with changes to

Fedora itself mean that institutions may have to revisit past choices. The Hyku FAQ page points out that if you want to move to Hyku later, it will become more complicated if you make any local customizations (Hyku Direct Archive, n.d.). Oregon State University had experience with this when its repository development team chose Sufia in 2015, and over the following years had to revisit with changes in the architecture. In ultimately landing on Hyrax 2.0 as the in-progress solution while it was still developing its own repository, the team was able to make its own local changes only by closely following the community conversation and being part of development (Tuyl et al. 2018). The fact that Oregon State wrote its project report for the Code4Lib journal in the structure of a Greek tragedy was, one suspects, not purely for rhetorical reasons. Nevertheless, members of the Samvera community reiterate in this article and in other spaces that success is not possible without being fully engaged in the community.

Types of Support Offered

Of all the projects in this book, the Samvera Community has one of the most well-defined community norms documented. The community principles are called "The Samvera Way," and are modeled on the Apache Way. The founding partners developed a Memorandum of Understanding for new partner institutions, and partners attend in-person meetings once or twice a year, in addition to e-mail discussions and phone calls.

The website and wiki have a clear explanation of all the avenues of support and collaboration available, including when to use the Samvera website, the GitHub repository, and the wiki. There are clear explanations of the community's governance and expectations, including a code of conduct. Finally, there is an explanation of how the community is sustainable over time, which is an important reassurance that the work won't go to waste (Branan 2017). Unlike other communities, Samvera never itself had a grant, rather relying on partner institutions to contribute back their own grant-funded projects, such as Avalon and Hyku.

Lessons to Learn

On the face of it, the Samvera Community is successful, and perhaps the best example of a large open source project in libraries that has maintained a strong and evolving community throughout the years despite its narrow focus as elements built on top of digital repository software. Its intentional approach to community and mix of formal structure and governance with the ability for anyone to participate in the community at some level allows for growth while maintaining necessary structure. Another factor in Samvera's favor is that it was always an international partnership. The United States and the United Kingdom have slightly different approaches to and incentives for open access to faculty research. As a result, products geared specifically for those uses will tend to drift into features that do not work outside that context. Given the need for more robust general-use digital repositories across all institution types, even those that have no need for an institutional repository, an international and widely distributed approach is more likely to reach consensus on solutions.

A decade into community building, the Samvera Community is looking to consolidate and retool what that approach is. This is partly to ensure that the community stays sustainable, and partly to convince decision-makers at partner institutions that this is an initiative worth funding year after year (Awre and Green 2017, 87). On the other hand, it remains the case that choosing to use Fedora and anything built on top of it means that an institution must take on a complex and expensive project. This is something that many institutions may be unwilling to do. For that reason, extending partnerships and community more widely beyond the seventy to ninety institutions represented in the community and at conferences may be a challenge.

■ Trove and the Digital Public Library of America

Although different in origin stories and approaches, these two projects are metadata aggregators that focus largely on the cultural heritage of smaller institutions (though certainly including larger institutions and corporate entities as well) across entire countries, Australia in the case of Trove and the United States in the case of DPLA. Rather than repositories themselves, these two projects bring together metadata from multiple repositories. To do so, they need to get those repositories to create metadata in a way that will work, as well as make their own platforms flexible enough to harvest the metadata. For this reason, some of the community give-and-take is more complicated than in other projects, as it requires a good deal of hands-on community management work to make this happen.

Origins, Challenges, and Current Status

Trove was started in 2008 as the "Single Business Discovery Service" by the National Library of Australia as a portal and metadata aggregator for various digital repositories, primarily for Australian newspapers, journals, and books. This addressed the technical challenge of maintaining multiple important research systems that dated back to the 1980s (Bryce 2014). It officially launched as Trove in 2009, and now includes pictures and photographs, government publications, music and video, maps, diaries and letters, and archived websites in addition to other materials (including those from HathiTrust). It opened its archives to crowdsourcing in late 2009 with the ability to tag items and create lists. Within a short period, however, the users had created their own set of rules for participating and what types of work they wanted to do.

Trove responded by making changes to its plans to meet the needs of the users, who so many years later are still active participants with a strong community. There are over 250,000 registered users, with around 9,000 active in a month, and millions of text corrections (Trove 2018). Trove is, in general, a flexible organization which has been used to taking collections from small Australian historical societies and adopting their idiosyncratic metadata into the larger standard system. Such an approach has meant that the tool could allow for innovative approaches over time (Ayres 2012).

The Digital Public Library of America (DPLA) makes a useful comparison to Trove, as an independent attempt to solve a similar problem. The initial planning for the DPLA began in 2010 with a grant from the Sloan Foundation. The idea was announced in an essay by Robert Darnton in the *New York Review of Books,* which asked "Can we create a National Digital Library?" (Darnton 2010). Because of examples like Trove, it seemed possible for the United States to achieve the same thing. Because there was not a national library, as such, to do the work, the DPLA organization at first created "workstreams" that were open to anyone to join in envisioning the process, which was to be partly a technical approach and partly a thoughtful curation approach (Heller 2012c). Just as with Trove, the DPLA works as a metadata aggregator, and requires metadata to be published in the public domain. That metadata is published by state or regional service hubs, which help smaller organizations get their metadata in a state where it can be harvested by DPLA.

Out of DPLA have come a few useful initiatives for the library community, such as RightsStatement, a collaboration with the Europeana digital library to define machine- and human-readable standard rights statements to facilitate harvesting digital objects. Going back to the Samvera project and Hyku, DPLA is one of the major collaborative partners in that project to make it easier for more institution types to have a digital repository.

Types of Support Offered

Trove offers an excellent example of fitting the task support to the needs of the members as they define them. Frequent communication about the status of the project both technically and from a management point of view provide context for development. The user community is active on a discussion forum provided by Trove, which includes detailed instructions on how to participate and comprises around 300 active members (out of a total of 30,000). Because much of the work is crowdsourced transcriptions rather than development, it is perhaps easier to train new members of the community. But without a strong sense of enjoyment and purpose, people will not remain committed. The community's emotional support means that the committed participants stay focused on their work and gain a reputation in their community, which Trove's Text Correction Hall of Fame honors. Such uses of the data could not have been predicted ahead of time, and the lesson is that communities should look to what committed members are doing and adapt to meet those needs.

From the beginning, the DPLA's community approach was attractive to librarians who, for example, enjoyed coming to hackathons held during the early planning stages (Heller 2012b). The DPLA community continues to this day, though without the same free spirit that characterized its early days. Yet it has initiatives such as an annual conference with opportunities to do innovative things with the data, and community representatives that help the public learn about the DPLA.

DPLA has well-defined documentation. It has user guides on its main site that gives its main identified user groups instructions on using the platform for needs such as genealogical research and scholarship, as well as the most basic information for developers (particularly those who come from outside the library community). On a separate site there are resources for the DPLA Professional Community that provide separate documentation for hub service providers, developers, educators, community representatives, and other groups. Layoffs and changes in focus in late 2018 have led to some questions about the future of community in the DPLA, however.

Lessons to Learn

Trove and the DPLA have much in common, though the origins and the way the collections have evolved their communities are different. The history of maintaining the Australian digital archives and need to continue—and perhaps slightly more stable funding of a national library—allowed the developers of Trove to take more risks and listen to the community more than a project with more uncertain funding or disparate developers. This seems counterintuitive based on what we tend to think about the slowness of governmental operations and may not be all that applicable outside of this context. But the willingness to watch what the community is doing and improve the product based on those practices is the essential lesson of open source development. Achieving flexibility within the parameters of the original mission is a challenge that Trove was able to meet.

■ Stability through Evolution

"Stability" will not mean that everything remains the same. What it means is that the community evolved appropriately to meet changing circumstances. These case studies show a variety of paths that projects can take over the years. After a decade, not all communities will still exist, and those that do will look different. Projects are not successful simply because they have lots of funding, the biggest institutional partners, or the most talented developers, though these things can certainly help projects that are otherwise successful. They succeed when they solve real problems in real ways that are compelling enough to maintain motivation over time.

Having star members or institutions may be helpful in securing funding but can hurt the project in the long term if this causes the community to lean too much on these for institutional memory and identity. Developing community means shaping the perception that everyone can contribute by facilitating that ability. This includes recruiting new voices and perspectives by helping people who do not see themselves as capable of participating in technology communities to feel comfortable.

Being intentional with community building means listening to the community and adapting with them. Ultimately, being mission-driven and making choices along the lines of that mission will ensure that people feel comfortable in making decisions and not feel that they are being exploited by participating—even if that means adapting the mission over the years as the community evolves.

CHAPTER 6

TECHNIQUES AND TOOLS

t this point it is time to look at some specific considerations for adopting support techniques and choosing specific tools to accomplish that support. These ideas can be used when starting out with a new community and choosing platforms or when reassessing current practices with an existing community. Although this chapter will not cover every eventuality for community projects, it will address the types of support and tools that many library technology projects already rely on to accomplish their work, and some general considerations for choosing techniques or tools.

Whose responsibility it is to choose the solution will certainly vary, but this could fall to the community manager, whether that is an individual or a group. Community management is about choosing the right tools and types of support to engage members. Successful communities may use the same tool in different ways: for example, the same mailing list software may be used for a technical discussion on one list, and for community building on another. Community managers, whether official or unofficial, may have to spend a significant amount of time experimenting with new ideas and adapting techniques. Note that many of the sections below are not about learning a specific piece of software, but about larger infrastructure decisions.

The following sections will refer to specific platforms, but it is a certainty that some of these will disappear and others will emerge. Testing out new platforms is often a fun challenge for technical communities and can be a good community-building hyphen if ad exercise. To avoid wasted effort, before testing a new platform, the community should spend some time discussing what the end goal is and document the results of the test. For example, a project management platform that is meant to help with developer coordination might end up working better for the people doing marketing and user support.

■ Starting a New Community

When you start working with others to create a new tool or start regular calls to discuss a new idea in library technology, taking a step back to think about the new community you have formed will save time in the end. It is not necessary to wait to begin work until everything is settled and all decisions have been made but making decisions deliberately will end up saving time later. We will go into the specific types of supports and the choices to be made with the tools and techniques below, but there are some general choices to be made.

Returning to the LYRASIS open source sustainability guide, this is the "Getting Started" phase of open source projects. In this phase, the most vital facets about which decisions must be made are technology and governance. Starting out with the best technical and governance decisions sets the community up for future flexibility to evolve. Choosing a name and a legal structure are two decisions that should be made early in the project. Although these both can and should be changed if necessary, they tend to be decisions with much longer-term ramifications than deciding which project management software to use.

Names

The need to choose the right name for a community may seem obvious, but this should not be done without thought. There are practical implications: for example, when the Samvera Community tried to trademark Project Hydra in 2016, they discovered that another technology project already had that name—and many other mythical creatures are already taken. The Read/Write Library Chicago, which formerly was the Chicago Underground

Library, needed to pick a new name when people heard "Underground" and made inaccurate assumptions about the collection. Because the library was already incorporated under the old name, this meant extra paperwork and potential confusion when the library assumed the new name. In both cases, these were solvable problems, but no one likes additional legal paperwork or cost, or the confusion that comes from changing names. Outsiders sometimes may assume that the name change was due to a change in mission or other consideration and not realize the project remains the same.

The ideological or rhetorical implications of the name are of equal importance to the practical issues in recruiting or maintaining potential members. When targeted to affinity groups, gender identities, or racial identities, it will be a challenge to choose a name that will clearly communicate the aim without dissuading potential members who are otherwise welcome. For example, the technology groups aimed at women in which I have participated have struggled with choosing a name that is not overly "feminine" or that seems to exclude those who are nonbinary. Care should be taken when using the word "librarian," because this could exclude library workers who are not librarians.

Names should ideally not be so unclear that potential contributors have no idea what the project does, though in fact many library technology projects have names drawn from other languages to ensure a unique name in English. Zotero is based on an Albanian word meaning "to learn something well," but as one linguist notes, the choice was not based on any actual connection with the Albanian language (Dingemanse 2008). Similarly, Omeka comes from a Swahili word that means "to display or lay out wares." Samvera is an Icelandic word meaning "togetherness," and many of the DPLA technologies have Icelandic names as well. These names are clever, but again, require a bit of thought to figure out how they apply. Spend some time thinking about the implications of borrowing words from other languages, how those names might be interpreted in English-speaking countries, and that they will not be offensive in other languages. This does not just go for the main name of the project, but for any acronyms that may derive from the name.

Legal Structures

Finding the right legal fit for an organization takes time and will need adjustment at some point should the project grow. What works for a small project with a few developers will not work for a major project with a budget and yearly legal requirements. Incorporating the organization officially has advantages, though the complexity and specific legal benefits vary by state and should be discussed with legal counsel. Spreading liability from an individual to an organization means greater safety for volunteers in the project. Licensing, trademarks, and other aspects of intellectual properly are particularly an issue for development projects. There are many different types of licenses under which software is released, and ensuring the project is meeting the legal requirements of those licenses should be a job for a board or steering committee. And should a project become self-sustaining through donations or other funding sources, having a legal entity that controls the money (and grants tax-free status) allows more oversight than entrusting individuals or institutions.

However, unless there are compelling reasons to incorporate right away (for instance, to satisfy grant requirements), there are other options for open source software projects to get legal and financial help. One example is the Software Freedom Conservancy, a not-for-profit organization designed to be a fiscal and legal agent for free and open source projects. There are many options for funding and sustaining open source software projects, and a number of organizations, such as associations, in the library world could potentially act as fiscal agents, depending on the needs of a community. Looking for existing structures such as working groups, interest groups, or other similarly informal groups within a larger organization could be a way to gain access to that organization's resources (technology, meeting spaces, mailing lists, etc.) while still maintaining some independence when making choices for the group members.

Code4Lib is an example of the legal evolution of a community. What had been a fairly small conference organized by different universities using the Code4Lib logo and organized by members of the group on the mailing list and wiki became a major conference with hundreds of attendees and increasingly complex finances that were not easy to pass over between universities from year to year. Choosing DLF as its fiscal agent made it possible for the conference to be more easily planned by many people in a certain region rather than at a single institution. Creating a new legal entity incorporated as Code4Lib with a governing board was never a popular option in the community, because it made a clear delineation about who would be "in charge," which would restrict the consensus-based or community-voting decision-making that made the group appealing to many people.

■ Code of Conduct

A code of conduct should be almost the first step after defining the mission and goals for the community, because it will codify how the mission and goals will be exemplified by the community members. A code of conduct sets the tone for participation and what type of behavior is expected and what is forbidden (e.g., harassment or name-calling). Codes of conduct may be particularly relevant in conference or group meeting situations but should govern all spaces in which the community exists, whether online or in person. Most importantly, it should lay out the specific actions that will occur as a result of a complaint, and have community buy-in for whomever helps enforce the code of conduct. It is critical that harassers who may have political capital in a community not also be given power to enforce community norms. Unfortunately, there is usually no way to know who those harassers are other than through a "whisper network," and so having some mechanism for confidential or anonymous reports will help to avoid dangerous situations. Although any adoption of a code of conduct will generate some amount of pushback and friction in a community, it is an important exercise to ensure that a community can effectively govern itself.

From a practical point of view, oftentimes speakers will not speak at conferences without a code of conduct. John Scalzi brought this to wide attention in 2013, but this matter is relevant to all types of meetings, including those of librarians (Brennan 2017). Another point of view holds that a code of conduct can be misleading to attendees because it will make it appear that some action will result from a violation report even when there is no plan in place (Spool 2014). However, for people who are new, outsiders, or uncomfortable in a community, it is critical to make it as clear as possible what the community's values are and how to get help (Nabors 2015). Of course, having a code of conduct without a plan to enforce it is not helpful, but that is no reason to avoid creating a code *and* an associated enforcement plan.

Writing a code of conduct is relatively straightforward because there are many models to choose from, including those used by existing library technology communities. The hard part is ensuring that the process of writing and implementing the policy works for the community. When a grassroots crowdsourced effort led by Andromeda Yelton resulted in the American Library Association adopting a code of conduct for conferences in 2014, reactions varied, which led to some loud disagreements and controversies in the library blogosphere.

The reactions ran along two lines: either that the process for creating the code of conduct should have been done in some more official manner, or that having a code was entirely unnecessary. The second point gets to the preceding discussion about the necessity for having a code so that expectations are explicit, and that a statement alone is not enough with clear enforcement stipulations, something that Yelton wished had been made more forceful in ALA's code (Yelton 2014), and has in fact proved to be an issue over the years.

The mechanism for creating a code of conduct ideally *should* be done by whatever the governing structure of an organization is at its inception. Whoever steps up to do the work should be supported. Karen Schneider pointed out that the ALA Council, some of whose members were upset that the document went up without Council approval, had failed to create a code of conduct previously, and so should not hinder the effort when made by others (Schneider 2014). The lesson from the creation of the ALA Code of Conduct is that library technology communities need a code of conduct to be one of the founding documents of the community, and that if someone comes into a community that lacks a code, it is entirely appropriate to ask the community to help create one. In her discussion of the controversy, Schneider adds that if she could have gone back in time to advise on the effort, she would have suggested building buy-in through more personal discussions with people on the ALA Council. As with all community governance discussions, dealing with the people involved will always be more challenging than writing the specific aspects of the policy.

TOOLS FOR THIS TECHNIQUE

- **Ada Initiative**: https://adainitiative.org/2014/02/18/howto-design-a-code-of-conduct-for-your-community/
  The Ada Initiative guide "HOWTO Design a Code of Conduct for Your Community" has a step-by-step guide to creating a code of conduct.

- **Geek Feminism Wiki**: http://geekfeminism.wikia.com/wiki/Code_of_conduct
  This wiki analyzes several community codes of conduct for potential issues and is designed to be a resource to accompany the Ada Initiative guide.

■ Project Management

Setting up or improving a system for project management will help communities work more efficiently. The work of project management is about ensuring that resources such as money, time, and personnel are allocated correctly. Anyone can do basic project management work, but project management is a profession all its own. The Project Management Institute is a professional body that certifies individuals with various types of expertise and specializations. Such expertise will be important for a large association or technical project that might have tens (or hundreds) of discrete projects going on at any one time. The work of managing dependencies between those projects will require another level of review. But even the smallest group of people getting together to solve a single problem will be more likely to succeed if some thought is put into managing the project ahead of time. No matter the scale of the project, someone should be paying attention to the overall status of the work and be ready to realign processes when they go awry.

A project plan should include, at minimum:

» what the project is intended to do
» what outcomes are within and outside the scope of the project
» who is involved in the project and in what roles
» who needs to be informed about the status of the work and at what stage
» the time line and dependencies for completing the work

This project plan should be addressed at every meeting and at other predefined review times and adjusted as new priorities or problems emerge.

Creating time lines and estimating the time it will take to complete a task is particularly challenging for projects that are a lower-priority task in a member's paid job or must be worked on in her spare time. Given this reality, it may be necessary to narrow the scope of the project and release it sooner, rather than increasing the time devoted to tasks or adding people to the project—Frederick Brooks' famous adage tells us that adding more people to a late project will just make it later. No matter the aspirations for a project, a useful technique from open source development is the idea of putting out a small but exciting deliverable that others can build upon or take in new directions.

Various tools exist to facilitate project management, and choosing the right platform depends on community preferences and characteristics. Complex software is available for detailed project management for large projects, but most communities do not need to start with anything too extensive. For smaller communities, a lightweight web-based tool should be sufficient, at least in the early stages. Some projects also may use a ticketing system or bug tracking system for managing technical work. Choosing a tool for managing the work of a community project cannot be an afterthought. Because the tools are designed to be flexible, it is important to come to a consensus on standards and workflow, and someone should be assigned to monitor incoming ideas or requests to ensure that they are categorized correctly. Note that there are many similar tools. I include here some that I have seen used in many library projects, most of which have roughly similar features.

TOOLS FOR THIS TECHNIQUE

- **Trello**: https://trello.com
  Trello uses "cards" on a "board." Boards are organized by stages of a workflow (or whatever else makes sense), and cards can contain detailed information about a task, images, tags, and subtasks. It can be used in a browser or via mobile apps. An Atlassian product, it is designed to integrate with other Atlassian products, though it can be used on its own as well. A useful feature of Trello is that boards can be public, which shows a project's progress and enables greater transparency. Trello is used by many libraries and librarians; for an example, see the public Trello board "Ultimate Idea Board: Ways to Use Trello in Libraries" (2017).

- **Asana**: https://asana.com
  Asana has a simple, primarily textual interface and can customize task layouts. Tasks can be in list or board format and can employ attachments and subtasks. Asana can be used in a browser or via mobile apps and has many built-in integrations to other software. Adding and working with tasks is very easy, making it a good option for small communities. It is available in a free version that limits the number of users and has fewer features (e.g., projects cannot be made public). The subscription version has more extensive features.

■ Documentation

Any technology project needs to have thorough documentation. From a technical standpoint, complete documentation is required so that the software will be maintainable and extendable. From a community-building standpoint, it helps to ensure that the project is accessible to newcomers. Successful community projects have documentation written for multiple types of users and at multiple skills levels. One way to accomplish this is by maintaining separate developer and end-user documentation. For larger projects, governance documentation will be essential, but it is worth including even for smaller projects where people need to know who makes technical decisions, and how. Making something happen technically as a user is a different consideration than the documentation developers require to extend the platform. A good example of this is DPLA's different portals for general users and professionals.

It may not be obvious at first exactly which types of documentation are needed. Personas or other user research may provide some clues about what to start with, but the goal of an open, extendable project will result in new ideas that cannot be predicted. For that reason, documentation should be created in such a way that writing, reading, and editing is straightforward and adding new information is easy to do at the point of need. However, waiting for the perfect system to come along should not preclude starting with whatever system will enable people to begin writing documentation.

The culture of documentation (i.e., how much value is given to it), as well as any lack of documentation in projects, are critical issues for participants in open source projects. The Open Source Survey found that nearly all participants had problems with incomplete documentation, and yet only slightly more than half had contributed to documentation. Note also that documentation that included contribution guides and codes of conduct was more valued by women (GitHub 2017). Creating documentation is a low barrier to entry for open source participation, and one of the easier ways to learn how to use version control systems.

For many projects, the documentation will be situated where the work is being done, but this may not always be the best choice, depending on the goals of the project. For example, if the code work is being done on GitHub, it would make sense to have the developer documentation maintained there, although that might be less accessible to technically inclined but non-developer users who might want to help write documentation.

A GOOD TOOL FOR THIS TECHNIQUE

- **Write the Docs**: https://www.writethedocs.org/guide
  The best source for learning to write documentation is Write the Docs, which is an international group of documentation advocates and educators. Its guide includes information on what documentation entails, how to write documentation, and how to create a culture of documentation.

Shared Documents

Using shared documents is a great way to get started with planning or idea sharing and can be a good way to store internal documents. For in-depth technical documentation or for documentation that needs to be accessed by many people there are some disadvantages for storing items in this way. Maintaining a usable structure and correct set of permissions can be challenging and navigating folder structures in some of these platforms can be cumbersome. For documentation that is meant to be public, considering a website-based platform (see below) may be more practical.

Shared documents can be created in many ways—a fully featured word processor, a simple text editor, or more specialized formats such as a spreadsheet or presentation slides. Online tools share common features including online hosting, the ability to be edited simultaneously, and mechanisms to set a range of permissions for editing. The major advantage to such tools is that the learning curve is low because most people are familiar with the interfaces and formatting doesn't require special syntax knowledge. It is usually possible to give varying levels of permission to read, write, or edit, as well as to track who made changes and at what time.

TOOLS FOR THIS TECHNIQUE

- **Google Drive/Docs**: https://drive.google.com
  Google Drive is a cloud-based file storage system that can store any type of file, especially those created in the various Google apps such as Google Docs, Sheets, and Slides. The advantage to using the Google apps is that because so many people have Google accounts, it is easy to give varying levels of permission to read, write, or edit, as well as to track who made changes and at what time, rather than opening a document up to anonymous edits (though that is possible). There are free versions of the apps, with paid plans available for additional storage space.

- **Microsoft Office 365**: https://www.office.com

  The web-based version of Microsoft Office, this platform is often available via an institutional license. Shared Word or Excel documents can be edited in real time by multiple people. Editing privileges can be extended to anyone with the link or limited to people in a specific institution using institutional accounts. Both personal and business plans that give access to Microsoft One-Drive cloud file are available at relatively low-priced tiers for annual plans. Although Office 365 can be more expensive than Google Drive/Docs, it is worth considering for shared documents, particularly those that will need to be shared or given to institutions that use Microsoft Office and where people may be most comfortable using that format.

- **Etherpad**: http://etherpad.org

  Microsoft and Google are certainly the big players in shared documents, but other options exist, and are worth considering for several reasons. For many people, the major advantage of this is the ability for potentially sensitive material to remain outside the large corporate ecosystem. One platform to consider is Etherpad, which is an open source collaborative editing tool that has public instances with encryption or can be installed on a private instance.

Web Platforms

Website-based platforms are ideal for established projects. Any website can maintain documentation. Maintaining user documentation on the project website in addition to code-specific documentation can be friendlier and look more "finished" to nontechnical users. This can be a flexible tool that has the advantages of built-in hierarchies or other desired features.

TOOLS FOR THIS TECHNIQUE

- **Hosted websites**

  Every community should have a web presence of some kind, ideally its own website with information about all the resources that support the project. There are multiple options for websites, from shared hosting services to a fully hosted option such as Google Sites, Wordpress.com, Blogger, or Squarespace. Choosing a platform will depend on the exact features needed for the documentation and the budget for the project: some are free, some have low-cost options. For most platforms, there are additional costs for adding a custom domain name and a security certificate.

- **Wikis**

    The main difference between a wiki and a website, in practice, is that wikis normally can use wiki syntax, which is a way of marking up text so it is formatted in HTML. They are also much more focused on tracking which user made which change. A website could be anything from plain text to a complex content management system. Because large technical projects are likely to already have websites, this may be an obvious place to document a project. The disadvantage of a website is that unless it has been set up correctly, it might be difficult to get permission to make edits and to track when edits were made. This is not impossible, however, and doing so will give the community the greatest amount of control.

- **Read the Docs**: https://readthedocs.org

    This is a free documentation hosting platform for open source projects, created by the Write the Docs community, and runs on either Sphinx or MkDocs (see below), with several choices for syntax. It is designed to be used in conjunction with a version control system so that documentation and code stay in sync and provides a browsable web interface as well as other formats such as PDF. It an excellent option for providing readable documentation for open source projects with code available in version control systems.

- **MkDocs**: https://www.mkdocs.org

    MkDocs can be used with Read the Docs, GitHub pages, or self-hosted. Documents are written in Markdown (a simple text editing format to turn text to HTML) and converted to a website using a Python program. While it takes some technical knowledge to get the program running, it is a straightforward tool for creating well-structured documentation.

- **GitHub**: https://github.com

    GitHub is a web platform for sharing and distributed development of code using the Git version control system. We will discuss Git and GitHub specifically as a version control solution, but for the purposes of documentation GitHub is another option. If the code is on GitHub, it makes sense for the technical documentation to reside as well. All GitHub projects have README files that show the steps to get the project running, which display right on the page. GitHub provides two additional venues for creating documentation. GitHub Pages (https://pages.github.com) is a fairly straightforward way to make a static website that can provide all the information about the project, including options to create a blog or other features. GitHub Gist (https://gist.github.com) is a way to provide code snippets to supplement other documentation where code may be harder to share. For example, you can put a code snippet on a Gist to support a conference presentation. An important caveat to using GitHub is that although people with a fair amount of technical proficiency should have no problem figuring out how to make edits and participate in shared documentation, it will be necessary to provide hands-on tutorials for how to participate, which other forms of shared documentation may not require. Just because the developers working on the project are comfortable doing everything on GitHub does not mean everyone else will be. Because learning version control systems is critical to moving ahead technically, offering as much training as possible and repeating it frequently will make more communities inclusive in the long run while also improving the documentation.

■ Discussion

Selecting methods for community discussions and deciding how they will be used will have many implications for the efficiency and inclusivity of communities. Discussion can be either technical discussion or community discussion; both help build engagement. The size of the project community may dictate whether it makes sense to have separate streams for technical or general discussion. Small communities with low-traffic lists most likely can use both. Another consideration is that it is likely that discussion will spring up in unofficial channels; if that discussion becomes toxic, it will hurt the community even if it is not officially community-sanctioned. For that reason, it makes sense to establish channels with community management in place ahead of time to ensure that the "fun" discussions can take place within the norms of the community.

Each of the platforms described below could theoretically be used for any type of discussion, but some will suit one type better than another. People will prefer to engage in discussions in a platform they already use, and in a method that best supports their work. For example, developers sharing code ideas are going to find platforms that support that more useful than a platform that is more geared to fun discussions.

TOOLS FOR THIS TECHNIQUE

- **E-mail lists**

  An e-mail list allows someone to send an e-mail to one address that will distribute the e-mail to everyone subscribed to the list. Subscribers can set their own preferences about when and how to receive the e-mails. Many people use "LISTSERV" as a generic term for e-mail mailing lists, though it is in fact a trademarked software that was first developed in 1986 and has been marketed by the L-Soft company since 1996. Many institutions do in fact run e-mail lists using LISTSERV, but there are a number of other options running on a variety of platforms. Operating a mailing list can be challenging from both technical and community management points of view. Ensuring that the software stays up-to-date, spammers are held in check, and discussions stay interesting and on track are issues that face mailing lists. However, mailing lists are the easiest point of entry because almost everyone has an e-mail address and some idea of how to handle e-mails. For small groups that lack access to mailing list software, other options may be a good place to start while they look for a host.

- **Facebook**: https://www.facebook.com

  Although Facebook may normally be thought of as a place to push out information about a project, it also is easy to create groups that can range from completely private and hidden to open and public; these are easy to set up and administer. Given how many people have Facebook accounts, this can be an excellent venue for emotional support, particularly for communities that are trying to reach outside the library world. There are a few potential problems with using Facebook, however. First, it requires that people have accounts under their real names, which may not be desirable or possible for some community members. Advertising may target members of the group. It may require individual members to open their personal lives to professional colleagues in a way that may feel uncomfortable or inappropriate. For those reasons, if a community is having more complex discussions or dealing with matters of governance, Facebook may not be the right venue.

- **Google Groups**: https://groups.google.com

  Google Groups is a Google service that allows for several types of online discussions. It can be set up as an e-mail list, an online forum, a Q&A forum, or a collaborative inbox. It is easy to set up and administer. Administrators can control how group members can interact with the group (e.g., whether they are required to use their real Google accounts or can use display names). Because this is straightforward and familiar to administrators and users, it is a popular option among communities, though those who wish to avoid Google will need to avoid this option.

- **Slack**: https://slack.com

  Slack is a popular messaging app designed for collaborative work, particularly for software development, thanks to its tie-ins with other platforms; for example, GitHub that allows code commits from within Slack. Slack is also fairly easy to use even for non-developers, and so is a good way for community collaboration between the community's technical and nontechnical sides. One useful feature of Slack is its channels, which can be used to keep work and personal discussion separate or to differentiate the discussions of subcommittees or working groups. Slack incorporates many other features that are useful for documentation and discussion such as file sharing and (for paid versions) voice calls and shared screens. Slack works best for groups that have a well-defined set of community norms because it has limited community management functions. Free versions of Slack have a 10,000-message archive.

- **Internet Relay Chat**

  Internet Relay Chat (IRC) is a text-based messaging protocol that began in 1988. It is based on a client-server model, and so requires an IRC server and a local client (which can be web-based). Among its advantages is the potential to be completely independent. However, getting started with IRC is more challenging than with other platforms mentioned. For anyone who wants to become involved in a more technical discussion or needs the independence that IRC channels can offer, it is worth taking the time to learn (and may be essential for getting involved with legacy projects). That said, for a new project with nontechnical participants, it should probably not be the first choice. For those with a strong interest in IRC, Freenode (https://freenode .net/project) is the best place to start. IRC has an estimated 90,000 users on 50,000 channels.

Video/Screen Sharing

For some decisions it may be preferable to communicate synchronously using options like video and screen sharing. This method has a few advantages. First, it allows people to get to know each other on a more personal level, which can help with communication and group identity when people may never meet in person—an added benefit for people who do not have time or ability to travel to participate in communities. Second, unlike text communication, it does not involve time lags that can hold up decisions or inhibit progress like those that occur when communicating via e-mail. Certainly, not every important decision needs to be made via synchronous communication—and some people have different comfort levels when speaking to others in real time, but in situations that may cause disagreement, setting up a call to talk "in person" can be helpful, this is still a viable option.

TOOLS FOR THIS TECHNIQUE

- **Google Hangouts**: http://hangouts.google.com
  Google Hangouts is a free tool with many useful features, including text messages, phone calls, and video calls with screen-sharing. It can be used on the desktop as well as through mobile apps. One feature that may be particularly helpful is "Hangouts on Air," which allows a Google Hangout to be viewed in real time and then archived on YouTube. (YouTube [2018] has several options for live events, including scheduling specific times and answering guest questions).

- **Zoom**: https://zoom.us
  Zoom allows people to set up meetings with up to one hundred participants and offers a desktop application, a mobile version, and an option to conduct meetings by phone. Its free tier limits meetings to forty minutes. The time limit and the inability to archive makes the free version less useful for important conversations, but as a free conference calling option it is better than some other free options. Search the web for "free conference calls" to find other tools, which are generally limited to voice calls.

■ Social Media

With hundreds of millions of active users, social media is ubiquitous, and whereas it used to be an optional feature for libraries and adjacent organizations it now is more-or-less required. The goal of social media is to have interactions within a community. Just as motivating volunteers requires understanding their motivations, choosing the right social media platform and communication style requires understanding whom you are trying to reach. For example, if you are trying to reach members of the public to encourage them to engage with a digital archive, a visual platform might make more sense. If you are trying to get professionals involved in an ongoing discussion about the goals of the community, a text-based platform will work better.

In all cases, it is critical to consider the ethical and legal ramifications when choosing a platform. At a basic level, read the terms of service and ensure that your community will not be harmed by those terms. Platforms disappear, and options change constantly. It is a good idea to maintain a local backup of content and any important statements made over social media are located elsewhere such as on the project website. Keeping track of changes in the social media zeitgeist could be a full-time job. As the use of platforms shift and new ones come out or close down (or simply become uncool), the community will have to make decisions about which platforms to maintain.

If you are starting from scratch, consider Twitter, Facebook, and Instagram (in that order). Depending on the community, you might consider Pinterest or Tumblr. Mastodon (https://joinmastodon.org) is a newer option that is a free open source tool for creating social media communities based on shared interests. In all cases, the responsibility for keeping the account active should be assigned to a designated individual or a committee. Social media committees can rotate on a monthly or weekly schedule, which will allow the account to have a personal "voice" without burning out a single person who has been designated to social media.

■ Version Control

Using version control tools allows multiple people to work on the same code or maintain multiple versions at the same time and later reconcile changes or pick the definitive version. No matter whether a single person or 300 people are working on the same text or code, someone is sure to make changes that are not a good idea or experiment with new ideas that may not be worth keeping. Learning the theory behind these tools and the methods for using them is a key skill for anyone who wants to learn software development and get involved in distributed development communities, but they also can (and should) be used by individuals for their own development work and can be also useful for nontechnical communities. For example, writing a code of conduct on a version control system allows voting on different versions of language as well as tracking who made which changes.

Each platform for version control uses a slightly different set of commands and syntax. Given that each project may use a different platform, it will be necessary to constantly learn and refine version control skills. Trying all the available version control systems is the only way to know which is the best for an individual project or to meet personal preference. The tools below are some of the most widely used, and all work in essentially the same manner. Either the command line or a graphical user interface is used to submit commands to start new branches of code, integrate changes, and explore differences in versions.

TOOLS FOR THIS TECHNIQUE

- **Git**: https://git-scm.com

- **Mercurial**: https://www.mercurial-scm.org

- **Bazaar**: http://bazaar.canonical.com
  Each version control language is separate from a code repository. Any language can be used on any system that supports it. Code repositories are sites that host code, usually the source code for software or a web application. Web-based applications may offer features like issue tracking, pull requests (i.e., to change something about the code), the ability to merge changes back in with the code, user profiles, and documentation. Some popular code repositories for library projects include:

- **GitHub**: https://github.com
  GitHub has free code hosting for public projects, and fee-based plans that offer private repositories and additional features suitable either for individuals or organizations. GitHub is used for many library technology projects, and having a GitHub profile, whether or not participating in a project, can be helpful for those who want to follow updates on other projects of interest.

- **GitLab**: https://about.gitlab.com

    A slightly newer company, GitLab has various levels of pricing and features, including a free tier with all the basic features required for hosting an open source project. One especially helpful built-in feature is continuous integration, which allows testing code as it is deployed. GitLab's interface emphasizes community. It can be hosted by GitLab or on a local server (the costs are similar either way).

- **Bitbucket**: https://bitbucket.org

    Bitbucket is a private Git repository manager created by Atlassian, and so is well-integrated with other Atlassian tools such as the Jira issue tracking system and Trello project management software. It has a free tier that accommodates private repositories with up to five users. As a service more focused on private repositories, it would not be appropriate for a widely distributed and open project, but for a project still in the planning stages or largely internally focused within an organization, it is a great option, particularly for Atlassian users.

■ Conclusion

Communities express their values through their statements and actions, which are exemplified in the choices they make for areas such as codes of conduct, documentation, discussion, outreach through social media and other channels, how projects undertaken by the community and version control are managed. When people feel they are respected, informed, and able to communicate, they are more likely to succeed. To achieve this, creating means for better communication should be the first step.

On the other hand, communities that have defaulted to the most widely used tools and which never discussed their choices should take time periodically to revisit the technical decisions they have made. As informal conversations begin that may lead to more in-depth work, it is a good idea to quickly review the tools for communication and documentation before too much effort is invested in the most convenient option. There is nothing wrong with choosing a convenient option, however, particularly if the community wants to recruit less technically inclined members.

CHAPTER 7

THE FUTURE OF COMMUNITY IN LIBRARY TECHNOLOGY

W e all want our work to have meaning and value, and one of the ways we measure that is by the relationships we have with colleagues. Sometimes these relationships result in a strong community within a workplace, while other times people wish to reach out beyond their organizations. No matter what, being intentional and thoughtful about creating communities not only helps us as professionals, it helps make our libraries better too.

We know that developing a strong library technology community requires the following steps:

» Identifying a problem and the people or institutions that need that problem solved.
» Understanding the motivations people have for getting involved.
» Engaging those motivations with appropriate work, tools, and channels.
» Selecting and monitoring those channels to ensure community norms are being followed.

This is a lot to accomplish, and not every project that fellows these steps will succeed. But success, when it comes, can result in great things for libraries. Moreover, we continue to benefit from the growth and adaptability of library technology over the course of its history. Library technology encompasses so many projects that are collaborative and community-driven because of the nature of preexisting library partnerships and the technological realities of the 1960s and 1970s. With the rise of free and open source software movements in the 1980s and 1990s, libraries were able to draw from them to establish collaborative technical partnerships to build software for libraries. As the nature of technology continues to shift, how should community technology projects prepare for the future?

■ Creating Community in Our Libraries

Good culture does not just happen. It takes work, and it requires that people come together into digital or online spaces frequently. Building camaraderie among the community members must be a formal expectation. The community must be founded on a code of conduct

I believe that the more we practice building communities in our professional lives, the more it will inspire us to build communities in our libraries. If we are used to treating our colleagues as partners for whom we care and whom we want to succeed, we can bring this same attitude beyond our professional lives. If we take careful note of how we support motivations and engage participants in a professional group, we can try the same techniques in our libraries. Of course, there are some special considerations for how we engage patrons, who likely will have their own, different motivations. Yet we can respect their needs for information and engagement, while having a mentality of partnership as service.

That mentality requires a well-chosen set of tools, but even more it requires respect for the potential contributions of each individual. The reason that people find a project like the Read/Write Library Chicago so compelling is that it explicitly invites each visitor to imagine her own work on the shelves of the library, and gives everyone a chance to try something, build something, to scratch his own itch. Trust and a willingness to accept risk and change are necessary to make this work, but when people are given that kind of respect, they usually rise to the occasion.

■ Taking It Forward

Communities cannot solve all problems, but I see the following points as the most important as we think about the future of communities in libraries. Some issues, such as a disparity in funding between, for example, large private research universities and rural community colleges, cannot be overcome entirely through community solutions. Yet even the largest private research universities will have a list of underfunded projects and institutional mandates that are impossible to meet with current resources. If even the well-funded institutions cannot keep up, this seems to me a missed opportunity to address systemic problems. Certainly, there have been many attempts to address these problems—but being too parochial in problem solving is not a winning proposition.

We probably do not want to build all our own solutions or rely completely on open source software. We can all agree that library vendors bring mixed blessings. The question remains: are we getting full value for our money? Developing a strong relationship with vendor representatives and support personnel will help to improve how we use products and receive necessary updates. Additionally, as we have seen, working with other customers to provide mutual support and coordinated enhancement requests is very worthwhile. Pushing vendors to open and embrace new modes of development—such as EBSCO's support of FOLIO—is one way that we can modernize our systems and keep prices more affordable overall.

There is no reason to avoid an open source development model; there are many benefits that come from that approach. On the other hand, communities have disappeared when the original developer could not foster a strong contributor base and there were not enough members to sustain the community. Libraries may consider using open source software for philosophical or cost reasons, but it is difficult to trust that the necessary tools will remain available or that those with less expertise will be able to use them. Tending to our communities' growth and maintenance will help libraries to be confident in the open source model.

The final takeaway is that communities will never be perfect. Documentation will be half-finished, meeting minutes will not get posted, and toxic people will join the board of directors. That does not mean that we cannot do a few small things to help our communities. Consider your experiences with library technology. Think about those communities that are most important to you. Identify one or two things you could do to fix or improve your community. If you are just beginning to work with open source or want to ensure the quality of the communities you are funding or sending your staff to, investigate what those communities offer by way of support. If you find what you need, ask for help. If that support does not exist, then you have found a niche you can fill to make that community stronger.

Aagaard, James S. 1987. "Computers and Northwestern University Library." http://notis-history.northwestern.edu/Computers.nul.htm.

Alfes, Kerstin, Amanda Shantz, and Catherine Bailey. 2016. "Enhancing Volunteer Engagement to Achieve Desirable Outcomes: What Can Non-Profit Employers Do?" *VOLUNTAS: International Journal of Voluntary and Nonprofit Organizations* 27 (2): 595–617. https://doi.org/10.1007/s11266-015-9601-3.

American Library Association. 2008. "History." www.ala.org/aboutala/history.

Apache Software Foundation. 2018. "How the ASF Works." https://www.apache.org/foundation/how-it-works.html.

ArchivesSpace. 2018. "Why Become a Member?" ArchivesSpace. http://archivesspace.org/community/why-become-a-member.

Avram, Henriette D. 1968. *The MARC Pilot Project: Final Report*. https://eric.ed.gov/?id=ED029663.

Awre, Christopher, and Richard Green. 2017. "From Hydra to Samvera: An Open Source Community Journey." *Insights* 30 (3): https://doi.org/10.1629/uksg.383.

Ayres, Marie Louise. 2012. "Digging Deep in Trove: Success, Challenge and Uncertainty." National Library of Australia. https://www.nla.gov.au/our-publications/staff-papers/digging-deep-in-trove-success-challenge-and-uncertainty.

Bankier, Jean-Gabriel. 2013a. "Talking about Digital Commons Development." *Digital Commons*.

———. 2013b. "Development Sneak Preview: January 2014." *Bepress* (blog). https://www.bepress.com/development-sneak-preview-january-2014-3/.

———. 2017. "Today's News." *Digital Commons*. https://groups.google.com/d/msg/digitalcommons/izthkqcYImY/03Yg-hfMAgAJ.

Barron, Anne. 2013. "Free Software Production as Critical Social Practice." *Economy and Society* 42 (4): 597–625. https://doi.org/10.1080/03085147.2013.791510.

Bitzer, Jürgen, Ingo Geishecker, and Philipp J. H. Schröder. 2017. "Is There a Wage Premium for Volunteer OSS Engagement? – Signaling, Learning and Noise." *Applied Economics* 49 (14): 1379–94. https://doi.org/10.1080/00036846.20 16.1218427.

Bourg, Chris. 2018. "For the Love of Baby Unicorns: My Code4Lib 2018 Keynote." *Feral Librarian* (blog). https://chrisbourg.wordpress.com/2018/02/14/for -the-love-of-baby-unicorns-my-code4lib-2018-keynote/.

Branan, Bill. 2017. "The Samvera Way: A Recipe for Success." Samvera - Dura Space Wiki. https://wiki.duraspace.org/display/samvera/The+Samvera +Way%3A+a+recipe+for+success.

Breeding, Marshall. 2016. "EBSCO Supports New Open Source Project." American Libraries Magazine. https://americanlibrariesmagazine.org/2016/04/22/ ebsco-kuali-open-source-project/.

———. n.d. "Library Technology Industry Mergers and Acquisitions." *Library Technology Guides*. http://librarytechnology.org/mergers/.

Brennan, Molly. 2017. "Why Your Meeting Needs a Harassment Policy." *PCMA Convene*, www.pcmaconvene.org/features/heres-what-to-include-in-your -meetings-harassment-policy/.

Brooks, Frederick. 2010. *The Design of Design*. Boston, MA: Pearson Education.

Bruns, Todd, Amy E. Badertscher, and Sheila Yeh. 2018. "It Takes a Community: Introducing the Bepress Advisory Board." https://works.bepress.com/ todd_bruns/70/.

Bryce, Catriona. 2014. "Trove—A Brief History." National Library of Australia. https://www.nla.gov.au/blogs/trove/2014/11/06/trove-a-brief-history.

Butt, Matti Ullah, Yu Hou, Kamran Ahmed Soomro, and Daniela Acquadro Maran. 2017. "The ABCE Model of Volunteer Motivation." *Journal of Social Service Research* 43 (5): 593–608. https://doi.org/10.1080/01488376.2017 .1355867.

CARLI. 2018. "History & Governance." https://www.carli.illinois.edu/about/ histgov.

Centivany, Alissa. 2017. "The Dark History of HathiTrust." In *Proceedings of the 50th Hawaii International Conference on System Sciences*. https://doi.org/ 10.24251/HICSS.2017.285.

Clary, E. Gil, Mark Snyder, Robert D. Ridge, John Copeland, Arthur A. Stukas, Julie Haugen, and Peter Miene. 1998. "Understanding and Assessing the Motivations of Volunteers: A Functional Approach." *Journal of Personality and Social Psychology* 74 (6): 1516–30. https://doi.org/10.1037/0022-3514 .74.6.1516.

Code4Lib Fiscal Continuity IG. 2017. "Fiscal Continuity." Code4Lib Wiki. https://wiki.code4lib.org/Fiscal_Continuity.

"Community Framework." Samvera. http://samvera.org/samvera-partners/community-framework/.

"Community Manager Job in Dublin—OCLC." https://web.archive.org/web/20180917021740/https://lensa.com/community-manager-jobs/dublin/jd/60c25ac6616877a8106538aa4b9e5c79.

Darby, Andrew. 2008. "Using Google Calendar to Manage Library Website Hours." *Code4Lib Journal*, no. 2 (March). https://journal.code4lib.org/articles/46.

Darnton, Robert. 2010. "A Library Without Walls." *New York Review of Books—NYR Daily* (blog), October 4. www.nybooks.com/blogs/nyrblog/2010/oct/04/library-without-walls/.

Della Bitta, Michael, and Kelcy Shepherd. 2017. "Progress and Future Plans for DPLA's Aggregator." Hydra-in-a-Box. http://hydrainabox.samvera.org/2017/12/06/aggregator-update.html.

Digital Public Library of America. 2018. "Welcome to the DPLA Professional Community." Digital Public Library of America. https://pro.dp.la/.

Dingemanse, Mark. 2008. "The Etymology of Zotero." *The Ideophone* (blog). http://ideophone.org/zotero-etymology/.

"Documenting the Now." n.d. DocNow. https://www.docnow.io/.

Dombrowski, Quinn. 2014a. "Steering/Curatorial Board." DiRT Directory. https://dirtdirectory.org/steeringcuratorial-board.

———. 2014b. "What Ever Happened to Project Bamboo?" *Literary and Linguistic Computing* 29 (3): 326–39. https://doi.org/10.1093/llc/fqu026.

DuraSpace. "DuraSpace History." DuraSpace. https://duraspace.org/about/history/.

ELUNA. 2018. "Product Development Agreement between Ex Libris, IGeLU, and ELUNA - ELUNA Document Repository." ELUNA Document Repository. http://documents.el-una.org/1236/.

Enis, Matt. 2016. "LYRASIS, DuraSpace Merger Dissolved." *Library Journal* 141 (11): 19–21.

———. 2018. "Virginia Tech First R1 Library to Adopt Koha ILS." *Library Journal*, http://libraryjournal.com/?detailStory=180814VTKoha.

Evergreen Project. 2013. "About Us." *Evergreen ILS* (blog). https://evergreen-ils.org/about-us/.

"FORCE11" FORCE11. https://www.force11.org.

Free Software Foundation. 2018. "What Is Free Software?" GNU Operating System. www.gnu.org/philosophy/free-sw.html.

Freeman, Daniel A. 2009. "SOLINET Executive Director Discusses SOLINET -PALINET Merger." ALA TechSource. www.ala.org/tools/article/ala-tech source/solinet-executive-director-discusses-solinet-palinet-merger.

GitHub. 2017. "Open Source Survey." Open Source Survey. http://opensource survey.org/2017/.

Google. 2018. "Create a Group & Choose Group Settings—Groups Help." https:// support.google.com/groups/answer/2464926?hl=en&ref_topic=2458761.

Gribbin, John H. 1988. *The Southeastern Library Network (SOLINET): A Topical History and Chronology, 1973–1983*. Columbia, SC: Association of South-eastern Research Libraries. https://library.oclc.org/digital/collection/ p15003coll197/id/147.

Harris, Laura. 2016. "Joining the Dark Side." *Against the Grain* 24 (2). https://doi .org/10.7771/2380-176X.6128.

Harris, Michael. 2017. *Solitude: In Pursuit of a Singular Life in a Crowded World*. New York: Dunne Books.

HathiTrust Digital Library. n.d. "Eligibility and Agreements." HathiTrust. https:// www.hathitrust.org/eligibility_agreements.

———. n.d. "Governance." HathiTrust. https://www.hathitrust.org/governance.

———. n.d. "Partnership Community." HathiTrust. https://www.hathitrust.org/ community.

———. n.d. "Technological Profile." HathiTrust Digital Library. https://www .hathitrust.org/technology.

———. 2011. "HathiTrust Personas." https://www.hathitrust.org/personas.

Heller, Margaret. 2012a. "Creating Quick Solutions and Having Fun: The Joy of Hackathons." *ACRL TechConnect Blog* (blog). http://acrl.ala.org/techconnect/ ?p=1443.

———. 2012b. "Report from the Digital Public Library of America Midwest." *ACRL TechConnect Blog* (blog). http://acrl.ala.org/techconnect/?p=2098.

———. 2012c. "The Digital Public Library of America: What Does a New Platform Mean for Academic Research?" *ACRL TechConnect Blog* (blog). http://acrl .ala.org/techconnect/?p=1478.

HathiTrust Research Center. "About the HathiTrust Research Center." HathiTrust Research Center Analytics. https://analytics.hathitrust.org/about.

"Hydra-In-a-Box." http://hydrainabox.samvera.org.

Hydra-in-a-Box Team. 2017. "Hyku Thank You." Hydra-In-a-Box. http://hydraina box.samvera.org/2017/11/21/thanksgiving.html.

"HykuDirect Archive." DuraSpace. https://duraspace.org/hykudirect/.

Jastram, Iris. 2018. "The Library Society of the World: Origin Story." *Pegasus Librarian* (blog). http://pegasuslibrarian.com/2018/04/the-library-society -of-the-world-origin-story.html.

Johnson, Richard. 1968. "A Book Catalog at Stanford." *Journal of Library Automation* 1 (1): 13–50.

Kilgour, Frederick G. 1987. "Historical Note: A Personalized Prehistory of OCLC." *Journal of the American Society for Information Science (1986-1998)* 38 (5): 381–4.

Klein, Michael B., and Julie Rudder. 2014. "Building for Others and Ourselves: Avalon Media System." presented at the Code4Lib National Conference. https://www.slideshare.net/AvalonMediaSys/avalon-code4lib-2014.

Lee, Yoo Young. 2017. "Who Are LITA Members? LITA Personas." *LITA Blog* (blog). https://litablog.org/2017/03/who-are-lita-members-lita-personas/.

LibTechWomen. 2014. "About LibTechWomen." 2014. http://libtechwomen.org/ about.html.

Lin, Gloria. 2016. "Masculinity and Machinery: Analysis of Care Practices, Social Climate and Marginalization at Hackathons." *Model View Culture* (blog). December 15, 2016. https://modelviewculture.com/pieces/masculinity -and-machinery-analysis-of-care-practices-social-climate-and-marginal ization-at-hackathons.

LYRASIS. 2016. "LYRASIS: Annual Report 2016." LYRASIS. http://lyrasisnow.org/ wp-content/uploads/2016/10/LYRASIS-FY2016-Annual-Report.pdf.

———. 2018. *It Takes a Village: Open Source Software Sustainability.* https://www .lyrasis.org/technology/Documents/ITAV_Interactive_Guidebook.pdf.

Margolis, Jane, and Allan Fisher. 2002. *Unlocking the Clubhouse: Women in Computing.* Cambridge, Mass.: MIT Press.

Matthews, Joseph R., Joan Frye Williams, and Allan Wilson. 1990. "Microcomputer-Based Library Systems: An Assessment." *Library Technology Reports* 26 (2).

McKenzie, Lindsay. 2018. "Educause Plans to Buy Assets of Bankrupt New Media Consortium." *Inside Higher Ed*, February 6. https://www.insidehighered .com/news/2018/02/06/educause-plans-buy-assets-bankrupt-new-media -consortium.

McSherry, Corynne. 2015. "Big Win for Fair Use in Google Books Lawsuit." Electronic Frontier Foundation. https://www.eff.org/deeplinks/2015/10/ big-win-fair-use-google-books-lawsuit.

Miller, Ron. 2016. "How AWS Came to Be." *TechCrunch* (blog). http://social.tech crunch.com/2016/07/02/andy-jassys-brief-history-of-the-genesis-of-aws/.

Nabors, Rachel. 2015. "You Literally Cannot Pay Me to Speak without a Code of Conduct." *Rachel Nabors* (blog). http://rachelnabors.com/2015/09/01/code-of-conduct/.

Nagy, Andrew. 2009. "Going Live!" VuFind News. https://sourceforge.net/p/vufind/news/2009/09/going-live/.

National Center for Education Statistics. 2007. "Digest of Education Statistics, 2007." https://nces.ed.gov/programs/digest/d07/tables/dt07_191.asp.

National Library of Australia. 2016. "Site News." Trove. https://trove.nla.gov.au/general/completedlist.

Neylon, Cameron. 2017. "Sustaining Scholarly Infrastructures through Collective Action: The Lessons That Olson Can Teach Us." *KULA: Knowledge Creation, Dissemination, and Preservation Studies* 1 (1). https://doi.org/10.5334/kula.7.

Noddings, Nel. 1984. *Caring, a Feminine Approach to Ethics and Moral Education.* Berkeley: University of California Press.

OCLC. 2015. "History of the OCLC Research Library Partnership." https://www.oclc.org/research/partnership/history.html.

———. 2017. "Mergers and Acquisitions." https://www.oclc.org/en/about/finance/mergers.html.

Ojala, Marydee. 2010. "PTFS Acquires LibLime, Expands Its Open Source Capabilities." *Information Today*, http://newsbreaks.infotoday.com/NewsBreaks/PTFS-Acquires-LibLime-Expands-Its-Open-Source-Capabilities-60726.asp.

OLE. 2018. "About." OLE: Open Library Environment. https://openlibraryenvironment.org/about/.

Parker, Ralph H. 1967. "The Small Library Faces the Future." *ALA Bulletin* 61 (6): 669–71.

Perry, Sara, and Nicole Beale. 2015. "The Social Web and Archaeology's Restructuring: Impact, Exploitation, Disciplinary Change." *Open Archaeology* 1 (1). https://doi.org/10.1515/opar-2015-0009.

Project Management Institute. 2018. "Certifications." Project Management Institute. https://www.pmi.org/certifications.

Ransom, Joann. 2009. "Liblime Forks Koha." *Library Matters* (blog). http://library-matters.blogspot.com/2009/09/liblime-forks-koha.html.

Raymond, Eric S. 1999. *The Cathedral and the Bazaar: Musings on Linux and Open Source by an Accidental Revolutionary.* Sebastapol, CA: O'Reilly.

Robertson, Tara. 2016. "Not All Information Wants to Be Free." *Tara Robertson* (blog). http://tararobertson.ca/2016/lita-keynote/.

Roy Rosenzweig Center for History and New Media. n.d. "Omeka—Project." Ome-
    ka. https://omeka.org/about/project/.
———. 2018. "Zotero Quick Start Guide." http://zotero.org/support/quick_start
    _guide.
Salmon, Stephen R. 1967. "Information Science and Automation: The Newest
    Division." *ALA Bulletin* 61 (6): 637–42.
Schneider, K. G. 2014. "Conduct Unbecoming (a Library Conference)." *Free Range
    Librarian* (blog). http://freerangelibrarian.com/2014/01/18/alacoc/.
Sessoms, Pam, and Eric Sessoms. 2008. "LibraryH3lp: A New Flexible Chat
    Reference System." *Code4Lib Journal* 2008 (4). http://journal.code4lib.org/
    articles/107.
Software Freedom Conservancy. 2018. "Software Freedom Conservancy." https://
    sfconservancy.org.
Specht, Jerry. 2014. "Interview of Velma Veneziano and Adele Combs." http://
    notis-history.northwestern.edu/Interview.JerVelmaAdele.htm.
———. 2017. "The NOTIS History Webpage." http://notis-history.northwestern
    .edu.
Spool, Jared M. 2014. "Safe Conferences Are Deliberately Designed." *Medium*,
    December 22. https://medium.com/@jmspool/safe-conferences-are
    -deliberately-designed-2849b6cd3658.
Syed, Christopher. 2011. *Parents of Invention: The Development of Library Automa-
    tion Systems in the Late 20th Century*. Santa Barbara, CA: Libraries Unlimited.
Trove. n.d. "Text Correction Hall of Fame." Trove. https://trove.nla.gov.au/news
    paper/hallOfFame?filter=newspaper.
———. 2018. "Statistics for Environment: Prod." Trove. https://trove.nla.gov.au/
    system/stats?env=prod#users.
Townsend, Robert B. 2013. *History's Babel: Scholarship, Professionalization, and the
    Historical Enterprise in the United States, 1880-1940*. Chicago: University of
    Chicago Press.
Tuyl, Steve Van, Josh Gum, Margaret Mellinger, Gregorio Luis Ramirez, Brandon
    Straley, Ryan Wick, and Hui Zhang. 2018. "Are We Still Working on This?
    A Meta-Retrospective of a Digital Repository Migration in the Form of a
    Classic Greek Tragedy (in Extreme Violation of Aristotelian Unity of Time)."
    The Code4Lib Journal, no. 41 (August). https://journal.code4lib.org/articles/
    13581.
"Ultimate Idea Board: Ways to Use Trello in Libraries." 2017. https://trello.com/b/
    eNTBqcvK/ultimate-idea-board-ways-to-use-trello-in-libraries.

Unger, Russ, and Carolyn Chandler. 2009. *A Project Guide to UX Design: For User Experience Designers in the Field or in the Making.* Berkeley, CA: New Riders Press.

University of Michigan Library. 2005. "UM Library/Google Digitization Partnership FAQ, August 2005." University of Michigan Library. www.lib.umich .edu/files/services/mdp/faq.pdf.

Veneziano, Velma, and James S. Aagaard. 1976. "Cost Advantages of Total System Development." In *The Economics of Library Automation: Papers Presented at the 1976 Clinic on Library Applications of Data Processing, April 25-28, 1976,* 13:133–44. Urbana, IL: Graduate School of Library Science. University of Illinois at Urbana-Champaign. https://www.ideals.illinois.edu/handle/ 2142/1075.

Villanova University Falvey Memorial Library. 2018. "About VuFind." VuFind. https://vufind.org/vufind/about.html.

Wen, Shawn. 2014. "The Ladies Vanish." *The New Inquiry.* https://thenewinquiry .com/the-ladies-vanish/.

Williams, S. 2017. "Sustainable Digital Scholarship." *On Archivy* (blog). https:// medium.com/on-archivy/sustainable-digital-scholarship-the-limitations -of-space-662627e19e37.

Yelton, Andromeda. 2014. "The ALA Statement of Appropriate Conduct: A FAQ." Across Divided Networks. https://andromedayelton.com/2014/01/02/the -ala-statement-of-appropriate-conduct-a-faq/.

_____. 2018. "LITA, ALCTS, and LLAMA Document on Small Division Collaboration – LITA Blog." *LITA Blog* (blog). https://litablog.org/2018/02/ lita-alcts-and-llama-document-on-small-division-collaboration/.

YouTube. 2018. "Live Events." YouTube. https://www.youtube.com/my_live _events.

t denotes tables